Lutino Greenfinch

Other titles of interest:

The Tropical Aquarium
Community Fishes
Coldwater Fishes
Marine Fishes
Maintaining a Healthy Aquarium
Garden Ponds
Aquarium Plants
Central American Cichlids
Fish Breeding
African and Asian Catfishes
Koi
Livebearing Fishes
Fancy Goldfishes
Reptiles and Amphibians
Hamsters, Gerbils, Rats, Mice and Chinchillas
Rabbits and Guinea Pigs
Pet Birds
Softbills

FINCHES

A pair of St. Helena Waxbills

Photographs by Cyril Laubscher

A pair of Jameson's Firefinches

A PETLOVE GUIDE TO

FINCHES

A detailed survey of this popular group of birds, with
practical advice on their care and accommodation

David Alderton

A *PetLove* Guide

© 1988 Interpet Ltd.,
Vincent Lane, Dorking,
Surrey RH4 3YX,
United Kingdom.

This (revised) edition produced for Interpet Ltd.
by Salamander Books Ltd.,
8 Blenheim Court, Brewery Road, London N7 9NT.

Heck's long-tailed Grassfinch

Credits

Editor: Vera Rogers   Design: Jill Coote
Colour reproductions:
Rodney Howe Limited
Filmset: Flairplan Photo-typesetting Ltd.
Printed in China

Author

David Alderton has kept and bred a wide variety of birds for over twenty years. He has travelled extensively in pursuit of this interest, visiting other enthusiasts in various parts of the world, including the United States, Canada and Australia. He has previously written a number of books on avicultural subjects, and contributes regularly to general and specialist publications in the UK and overseas. David studied veterinary medicine at Cambridge University, and now, in addition to writing, runs a highly respected international service that offers advice on the needs of animals kept in both domestic and commercial environments. He is also a Council Member of the Avicultural Society.

Photographer

Cyril Laubscher has been interested in aviculture and ornithology for more than thirty years and has travelled extensively in Europe, Australia and Southern Africa photographing wildlife. When he left England for Australia in 1966 as an enthusiast aviculturalist, this fascination found expression as he began to portray birds photographically. In Australia he met the well-known aviculturalist Stan Sindel and, as a result of this association, seventeen of Cyril's photographs were published in Joseph Forshaw's original book on Australian Parrots in 1969. Since then, his photographs have met with considerable acclaim and the majority of those that appear here were taken specially for this book.

Contents

Introduction 10

Buying and handling finches 12

Housing 16

Feeding 36

Breeding and rearing 46

Health care 58

Species section 64
A photographic survey of over 50
popular finches

Index 114

Further reading 116
Picture credits 117

Page 10–11 *Red-crested Finch*
Page 64–65 *Orange-cheeked Waxbills*

Introduction

Strictly speaking, the ornithological description of 'finch' is applied only to birds grouped in the family Fringillidae. In birdkeeping circles, however, the term refers to a much wider range of birds and is used as a practical description to identify their feeding preferences. In this sense, finches are birds that feed primarily on seed, and they are also sometimes known as hardbills. This distinguishes them from the so-called softbilled birds, which need a much higher proportion of fruit, insects and softfoods in their diet if they are to thrive in captivity.

The division between finches and softbills is not mutually exclusive, however, especially since some finches, such as buntings, require a relatively high proportion of softbill foods as part of their daily diet. Furthermore, many finches become highly insectivorous when they have chicks in the nest, and you must modify their diet accordingly during the breeding period.

It is the lively nature, attractive coloration and the ease of maintaining and breeding finches in a variety of domestic situations that make them so appealing. Since they are not noisy – and some even have an attractive song – finches are ideal occupants for the garden aviary in an urban area. The aviary can become an attractive focal point in the garden, with plants providing both nesting sites and insect life for the occupants.

Finches are quite inexpensive to buy and maintain, which makes them an ideal choice for young and old alike. In spite of their small size, they may live for well over a decade in domestic surroundings. In the first part of this book we discuss the practical aspects of keeping finches, including the points to look for when choosing birds, and how to house and feed them. The final sections in Part One offer advice on breeding and rearing finches and consider health problems that you may encounter.

Buying and handling finches

Finches are available from various sources and where you buy your birds depends on your requirements. If you simply want to set up an aviary for finches, then your local pet store may well be able to supply you without any difficulty. However, if the exhibition side of the hobby appeals to you, then it is best to contact successful exhibitors in order to obtain the best stock you can afford. To find some of the more unusual and costly finches you may have to approach the specialist outlets, such as bird farms or private breeders. The advertisement columns of the specialist avicultural magazines will give you a guide to the current prices being asked for a particular species or mutation and likely sources of supply.

Choosing young stock

It is virtually impossible to age finches reliably once they have attained adult plumage, but their legs may provide a clue. If these are heavily scaled, the individual concerned is probably not a young bird. Domestically-bred stock may be ringed with a closed circular band, which provides a guarantee

Below: *Be sure to buy young and healthy birds. If exhibiting appeals to you, seek out a specialist breeder for stock and practical advice.*

of the bird's year of hatching. In addition to this information, the ring may carry a sequential number, and the breeder's initials and club details may also be included.

In the long term, there is much to be said for acquiring young finches. Hopefully they will have a longer lifespan and 'current-year bred' youngsters will be able to settle in their quarters before being expected to nest in the following year. From the exhibition standpoint, few breeders will dispose of their best breeding pairs, but they may be tempted to sell some of their youngsters. This can have obvious advantages when you are in the process of setting up your own stud of birds. Try to be as familiar as possible with the show standards for the variety concerned, however, so that you have a sound understanding of the strengths and weaknesses of the finches on offer.

Choosing a healthy bird

Before you buy a bird, you will want to be certain that it is in the best of health and you should examine it carefully. Young finches housed in a cage should be lively, moving readily back and forth from perch to perch. The bird's plumage should be tight, but do not be too worried by the condition of the plumage, since this will be replaced at the

Above: *Black-headed Gouldian with an immature individual (inset). Only with young stock can you be sure of a bird's age. Always check the bird's body weight carefully.*

next moult. At breeding time some cocks moult into nuptial plumage and are advertised as 'I.F.C.' (In Full Colour) as distinct from 'O.O.C.' (Out of Colour). In overcrowded conditions, the birds may pluck each other, especially around the head, but the feathers will regrow when the birds are moved to more spacious surroundings.

Check that the eyes are clear and show no signs of a discharge, which may be the result of a minor infection, possibly acquired from dirty perches. On the other hand, the condition of the eyes may indicate a more serious ailment. A sick bird, for example, will often huddle on its perch with its eyes closed for long periods.

You can assess the overall condition of the bird from an examination of the breastbone, located in the midline on the lower part of the body. Under normal circumstances, this bony prominence should be apparent just as a slight projection, with no hollows on either side. A pronounced gap is indicative of a condition described as 'going light', which is especially common in young Gouldian finches and greenfinches (see page 60). Although 'going light' is a symptom, rather than a specific disease, it is highly probable that the bird is suffering from a chronic illness and successful treatment may not be possible.

Examine the beak and claws for any deviations and avoid buying a bird with any malformation of the beak. If the claws are overgrown they can be cut back. Indeed, it is not unusual for certain finches, such as various weavers, to have relatively long and spindly claws.

Above: *A Chestnut-breasted Mannikin with overgrown and twisted claws. Regular clipping is essential for some finch species.*

These can prove hazardous, since they may cause the finch to become caught up in its surroundings and they will need regular clipping (see page 63).

The condition of the feet is especially important if you are looking for show finches. Any missing claws will be penalised, so make sure that the birds you are buying have the full complement. The loss of a claw will not handicap the bird, however, and such finches will breed normally.

New arrivals

Finches acquired in winter will have to be kept indoors until the following spring, unless they are being transferred directly from one outside aviary to another. Imported birds are best housed in indoor accommodation for their first winter, although in mild areas it may be possible to leave them in an aviary. Recently imported finches will not be acclimatized, however, and will have to be kept in heated surroundings before they can be transferred to an outdoor aviary. Wait until the weather is favourable and any threat of frost has passed.

For this reason, the best time of year to acquire stock is in the late spring or early summer.

Even if you do not have access to a garden, it is possible to keep and breed finches indoors without problems. Although they will not become tame, or learn to talk like a budgerigar, for example, finches settle down well in an indoor flight. In any event, you may prefer to house them in this way during the winter months.

It is a good idea to keep new finches in a cage for a week or so, to ensure that they are eating properly and remain healthy. This is especially important if you are introducing new birds into an existing aviary. The newcomers will be able to recover from their journey, and the likelihood of introducing sick birds alongside the established finches is significantly reduced. Try to ensure that new birds are released into the aviary before the breeding period, otherwise they may be persecuted by the established occupants.

If you are introducing finches into an unoccupied aviary, confine them in the shelter for the first few days after their week in the cage so that they can become familiar with the arrangement of the feeding pots here. (Once a group is established, newcomers tend to follow others to the food pots.) Placing the perches within the shelter in a slightly higher position than the perches in the outside flight will encourage the birds to return to roost here once they are released into the outside flight. This is especially important as the nights get colder, although some finches still insist on remaining in the flight despite all attempts to induce them to roost inside the shelter.

Catching and handling finches

The beaks of most finches are not sufficiently powerful to cause you any discomfort should they bite. There are a few exceptions – notably hawfinches – and it may be advisable to wear thin gloves when handling these particular birds. It is much easier to catch finches in the confines of a cage than in an aviary, since these birds can prove exceptionally agile in flight. If the bird is in a cage, simply put one hand through the door and use the other hand to ensure that the bird cannot slip out through the opening. You should then be able to take hold of the finch without difficulty, especially if you first remove the perches.

Once you have the bird in your hand, be sure to keep it adequately restrained, with its wings folded in the palm of your hand. It is less likely to struggle under these circumstances. You can hold the bird's head in the circle formed by your thumb and first finger, or support it between the first and second fingers. This latter method is preferable; with the head in this position you will be able to examine most of the body, including the beak, breastbone and feet without difficulty. Take particular care to ensure that your fingers merely support the bird's head and do not compress its neck, since squeezing the windpipe could obviously interfere with the bird's breathing.

Below: *Restraining a Red-headed Gouldian carefully in the hand. Never grip finches tightly – they do not inflict a painful bite.*

Catching finches in an aviary is likely to create a disturbance and you should not attempt to do it if at all possible when any birds are breeding, as they may desert their nests. If you must remove a bird, confine the finches in the aviary shelter, using the sliding hatch for this purpose. Away from the clutter of plants in the outside flight you can catch them more easily.

In a large area it is possible, but difficult, to catch finches in flight with a catching net, well-padded around the rim. Instead try to place the net over the bird when it has alighted on the floor or on the aviary mesh. Alternatively, you may find it easier to catch the bird with your hand. In either case, move slowly at first, and always be very careful when using a net, since even a net with a padded rim can injure the finch if you accidentally hit it hard.

Catching and handling finches is largely a matter of practice. If you have difficulty, and a bird starts to breathe heavily and becomes very distressed, leave it alone to recover, rather than risk upsetting it further. In reality, there will be few occasions when you need to catch the birds; you may have to do it only once a year when you are transferring them indoors for the winter, for example.

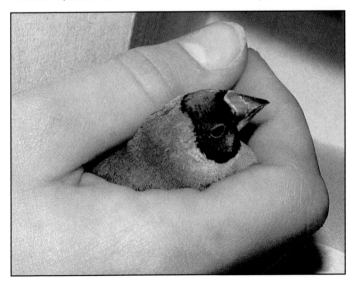

Housing

Finches are relatively easy to accommodate, since they will not damage the structure of their quarters, and aviaries of many shapes and sizes will be suitable for them. The birdkeeper's main consideration must be how best to keep these small birds over the winter and this decision will be influenced by the prevailing weather conditions in your area. In mild localities, where the average temperature is unlikely to fall below freezing and day length is relatively constant, a basic aviary will be adequate. In temperate climates, including parts of Europe and North America, the winter weather can prove too inclement for finches to be housed out of doors without the provision of artificial heating and lighting. Always consider these requirements carefully when designing and constructing an aviary for these birds. If you have a small collection of finches it may be feasible to bring them indoors for the duration of the winter.

Aviary components

An aviary usually consists of two parts; an outer area – or flight – constructed of wired panels, and a shelter, where the birds feed and retreat during bad weather. A typical flight is about 270cm(9ft) long, 90cm(3ft) wide and 180cm(6ft) high. It is easy to work in a structure of this size, although for individual pairs of small finches the flight length is often reduced to 180cm(6ft).

It is possible to run several small flights in parallel off a single large flight. By expanding the shelter to incorporate cages and indoor flights, you create a birdroom. Although more costly, this type of structure is certainly recommended for finches, since it can provide accommodation during the winter, and facilities for breeding and training exhibition stock.

You can buy panels in kit form to assemble into both a flight and a shelter, although you will probably need to look at one of the specialist birdkeeping periodicals to find a supplier. Alternatively, your local pet store may be able to provide a contact, although, generally, pet shops do not sell aviaries. More specialist outlets concentrating on the sale of birds and accessories may have assembled aviaries on view and it is well worth travelling to look at different aviary designs and the standard of workmanship.

Below: An aviary for finches can become an attractive garden feature. Note the safety porch shown on the front here, and the snug roosting quarters on the left.

Above: *A striking octagonal flight with an internal shelter. Be sure to provide adequate weather protection on the exposed panels.*

You can choose to buy a complete aviary, or plan your own using the various components in a standard range of panels. This is a more versatile option and allows you to expand the structure more easily at a later stage. Most firms operate a design service, so if you provide a rough sketch of the aviary that you envisage, they will draw up a list of the necessary component panels. It should be possible to arrange for the panels to be clad with 1.25cm(0.5in) mesh, although this will cost extra. Find out whether the woodwork is treated with a weather-proofing compound. This prolongs the lifespan of the structure, but is charged as an extra by some aviary manufacturers.

Siting the aviary
It is important to ensure that the finished structure is an attractive garden feature, designed to blend in with its surroundings. Before you start work, it is as well to find out whether you need official permission to construct an aviary. In most instances, planning approval is not required, especially if the structure is small.

You should consider a number of factors before deciding on the site of the aviary. A location at the back of the house will ensure that the structure is screened as much as possible from neighbouring roads. Here, the birds will not be disturbed by car headlamps after dark – which can cause them to desert their nests – and the structure itself will be less accessible to vandals.

Try to choose a sheltered spot, so that the birds will not be exposed to the prevailing wind and driving rain. Avoid siting the aviary beneath trees; although trees can screen the roof, leaves are likely to accumulate here and falling branches may damage the structure, as well as frighten the birds within.

Choose a quiet spot in the garden. If younger members of the family regularly use an area of lawn for ball games, for example, site the aviary as far away as possible from this area of activity. If possible, find a site where the aviary is clearly visible from the house, so that you can enjoy watching the birds even when you are indoors. A site close to the house also has practical advantages since it will be easier and less costly to extend a power supply to the aviary for heating and lighting purposes.

Consider the size of the structure

carefully and, ideally, choose an area that will allow room for expansion at a later stage. You may prefer to have several smaller flights, housing just one or two pairs of finches of the same species, rather than a larger communal flight, with several species housed together, as breeding results are likely to be better with certain species under these conditions.

Preparing the site

Whether you buy an aviary in kit form or build one from scratch, you will have to prepare the site and construct footings for the structure.

First of all, clear the site and cut any turf that you wish to keep into sections. Store these in a cool spot in the garden and, providing the turf is kept damp, you can use it to landscape the area at a later stage.

Level the ground if necessary, and stake out the dimensions of the aviary so that you can prepare the foundations. A secure base is essential, not only to ensure that the aviary is stable, but also to exclude vermin. Setting blocks in

Below: A simple aviary design assembled from a kit available from specialist suppliers. Prepare firm foundations for aviary structures.

the ground to a depth of about 30cm(12in) around the perimeter will help to prevent burrowing creatures, such as rats and foxes, from entering the aviary and seizing the occupants.

The trench for the footings should be approximately twice the width of the blocks. Mount the blocks on a bed of mortar and hold the soil back, by shuttering if necessary, so that it does not collapse into the trench. Mark the division between the shelter and the flight with another course of blocks, corresponding in height to those marking the perimeter.

Extend the blockwork for about 30cm(12in) above ground level as well. This will ensure that the wooden framework of the aviary is not in direct contact with the soil, or splashed by the rain which will cause it to rot prematurely. You can face the blockwork with mortar, and then cover the mortar with an exterior paint to create an attractive finish. Alternatively, you may prefer to use brickwork above ground level, in place of blocks.

One of the most significant decisions you will have to make concerns the floor covering of the flight. Obviously, a planted flight will be more attractive than a bare aviary with a concrete floor, and it

may also contribute to breeding success. But careful planning is required, especially if the aviary is relatively small. Under these circumstances, the best option may be to confine all the plants to tubs and pots on a base of concrete or paving slabs.

To prepare a concrete floor, dig out the soil as necessary and put in a layer of well-compacted hardcore at least 15cm(6in) thick. Cover this with a mixture of ballast and cement to a similar depth. When it has dried, prepare a final covering of sand and cement to give a smooth surface on top. At this point, it may be worth seeking the help of a plasterer, who will create not only a smooth surface, but also a slight slope to the base, so that rainwater will run off rapidly and not accumulate on the aviary floor. The water can be channelled out of the flight via a piece of narrow bore plastic tubing set at the appropriate level in the base. Drainage is especially significant in a flight for finches, since there is always a risk that these small birds – especially newly fledged chicks – could become waterlogged and even drown on the floor in a heavy downpour. Be sure to allow the concrete floor to dry thoroughly before erecting the flight panels.

If you choose paving slabs, they will need to be laid just as carefully to achieve good drainage. Fill the gaps between the slabs with mortar. One advantage of using slabs rather than concrete is that they are less likely to support algal growth. This can look unsightly, especially after the winter, but it is not a major problem, since it is easy to scrub off the greenish deposits.

Building your own flight
You do not have to be an expert carpenter or builder to construct a flight. The best time to start work is in the spring, when the weather is likely to be favourable. The early building stages can be undertaken in a garage or workshop, but constructing the frames is best carried out in the garden because of the space required.

Even though finches are not destructive birds, their quarters should be solidly constructed. Flight panels should be jointed, rather than simply nailed together, otherwise the timber may become twisted over a period of time. If the framework becomes badly distorted, birds may disappear through the small gaps.

You will save a lot of time if the lengths of timber are cut to the appropriate length before delivery. Plan the flight frames to correspond as closely as possible to the width of the mesh that will be used to cover them. This is usually 90cm (3ft) wide. Mesh which is 180cm(6ft) across may appear to offer a saving in terms of timber, but it will tend to sag on the frames once these are assembled and detract from the finished appearance of the aviary.

It is a good idea to use timber that has already been treated with a weather-proofing agent or you may prefer to place the lengths of timber on trestles and paint them with a suitable preservative. Apply at least two coats of preservative and leave the timber to dry thoroughly before assembling the frames. In the case of pre-treated timber, it will only be necessary to paint the cut ends to protect them against the elements.

The dimensions of the timber will obviously have a bearing on the cost of the aviary. For indoor flights (see page 26), it is certainly possible to use 2.5cm(1in) square timber. However, a more solid structure will result if you use 3.75cm(1.5in) square timber for the external framework. This provides a wide surface over which to attach the wire, and lessens the strain on the individual netting staples.

Once the lengths of timber have been jointed, assemble the individual panels using screws to produce a sectional structure. With careful maintenance over the years, this structure can be dismantled and moved, or even expanded.

The next stage is to attach the wire mesh to the frames. You may prefer green plastic-coated mesh, which is more durable than galvanized mesh and also makes it easier to see the birds in the flight. Mesh is sold according to size and thickness, or gauge (G). A thin gauge will be adequate for finches: 19G is ideal, although 22G – which is finer and slightly cheaper – is occasionally used for flight panels. The advertisement columns of birdkeeping journals usually carry details of discount suppliers of aviary mesh for the DIY market.

It is best to use 1.25cm(0.5in) square mesh for the flight panels of the aviary. Many ready made aviaries are constructed using 2.5x1.25cm (1x0.5in) mesh, which will contain most finches but, unfortunately, also allows mice and other creatures to enter the aviary. These animals will inevitably upset

A large aviary

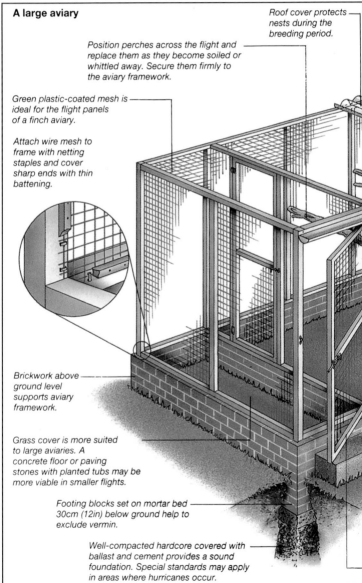

Roof cover protects nests during the breeding period.

Position perches across the flight and replace them as they become soiled or whittled away. Secure them firmly to the aviary framework.

Green plastic-coated mesh is ideal for the flight panels of a finch aviary.

Attach wire mesh to frame with netting staples and cover sharp ends with thin battening.

Brickwork above ground level supports aviary framework.

Grass cover is more suited to large aviaries. A concrete floor or paving stones with planted tubs may be more viable in smaller flights.

Footing blocks set on mortar bed 30cm (12in) below ground help to exclude vermin.

Well-compacted hardcore covered with ballast and cement provides a sound foundation. Special standards may apply in areas where hurricanes occur.

the finches and may harm them directly or introduce disease.

Use netting staples to attach the mesh securely to the framework. You will need plenty of space for this operation, so work in the garden, preferably on a flat surface. Start at the top of the frame and carefully unroll the mesh over the full face of the panel. Place two netting staples at the top corners of the frame. Then pull the mesh down tightly, ensuring that it runs in a straight line and remains taut over the rest of the frame. You can hold the mesh in place with blocks, but it is usually better if you can get someone else to grip one end while you fix the mesh in place, working down the sides of the frame.

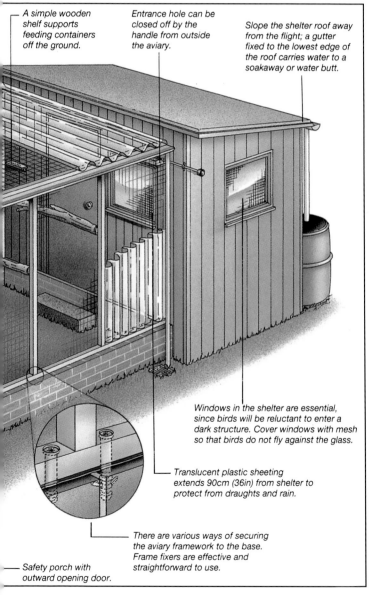

A simple wooden shelf supports feeding containers off the ground.

Entrance hole can be closed off by the handle from outside the aviary.

Slope the shelter roof away from the flight; a gutter fixed to the lowest edge of the roof carries water to a soakaway or water butt.

Windows in the shelter are essential, since birds will be reluctant to enter a dark structure. Cover windows with mesh so that birds do not fly against the glass.

Translucent plastic sheeting extends 90cm (36in) from shelter to protect from draughts and rain.

There are various ways of securing the aviary framework to the base. Frame fixers are effective and straightforward to use.

Safety porch with outward opening door.

Be very careful when you cut the roll free, since the loose cut edges of a 30-metre(33-yard) roll of mesh may spring upwards with surprising force. Wire cutters are most effective for the task, although you can use a hacksaw instead. Add in extra netting staples at this stage, so that the mesh is firmly attached around the perimeter of the wooden frame. Finally, cut lengths of thin battening 2.5cm(1in) wide and attach these to the top and bottom of the framework. These will cover the sharp ends of mesh, which might otherwise injure the finches once the flight is assembled. Mark each frame as it is completed, so that you know where it fits within the flight.

The safety porch

Finches are very quick on the wing and a safety porch should be an integral part of their aviary to ensure that there is no risk of any birds escaping when someone enters the aviary. The porch need not be an elaborate structure and can be constructed in an identical way to the flight. The typical dimensions of a safety porch are about 90cm(3ft) square and 1.8m(6ft) high; this should allow easy access to the aviary. Hang the door of the safety porch so that it opens outwards, away from the aviary. This will give you space to store cleaning equipment, such as brushes and buckets inside, and you will also be able to enter and close the door. Secure the safety porch door with a sturdy sliding bolt attached to the inner face.

You must also decide on the arrangement of doors within the aviary. The door from the porch to the aviary should open inwards, either into the shelter or the flight. Direct access to the shelter is more important since this is where the birds are fed. It should not be necessary to walk through the flight each day in order to feed the birds, since this constant activity on your part may cause them to desert their nests during the breeding season. If you opt for direct access to the shelter, there is no need for a separate entrance into the flight, since you can enter it via a door leading from the shelter.

Protection from the elements

The birds will need protection from the worst of the weather when they are in the outside flight. Translucent plastic sheeting fitted along the mesh and extending at least 90cm(36in) from the shelter will protect them from draughts and driving rain. At the onset of the breeding season, you may also need additional cover over the roof of the flight to protect the nests from flooding, which will cause losses both of eggs and chicks. Where the overhead plastic sheeting finishes, fix up guttering to carry away the rainwater so that it does not pour into the flight.

It is advisable to place plastic sheeting around the back of an octagonal aviary, especially if the shelter is sited in the centre of the structure. These ornate designs certainly look attractive, but without additional protection they can be rather exposed to the elements.

Building a shelter

You can construct a shelter from scratch, using the same basic framework as for the flight. Be sure to design the roof so that it slopes towards the back of the shelter, enabling rainwater to run off it. Fix guttering to the lowest edge of the roof to carry rainwater to a soakaway or waterbutt. If your shed has an apex roof, you will need guttering on both sides. Clad the sides with either tongued-and-grooved boarding, or external plywood. Boarding looks more attractive, but both are effective draught excluders. You can stain the timber on the sides of the shelter to the required shade. The roof section is best made of plywood, and should extend out over the sides of the shelter.

Small shelters

As timber costs have risen, there has been a trend towards building less elaborate covered accommodation. Instead of a full-height shelter, which permits easy access, a raised box-type of structure has become more commonplace. This may be incorporated into the flight itself or built outside it. The first option is preferable, since it affords greater security and it is still possible to service the interior from a surrounding safety porch without difficulty. If the shelter is built outside the flight, however, you will need to extend the structure of the safety porch beneath it, to close the gap at this point.

It may be possible to enter the flight by incorporating a door beneath the raised shelter, so that only one safety porch is required. This is difficult, however, and a separate access at the other end of the flight is usually recommended under these circumstances. Bear in mind that two routes of entry will add to the cost of the structure and, with accompanying safety porches, take up more space in the garden.

It is sometimes suggested that under these circumstances you can dispense with safety porches, simply by positioning the access doors low down. It is true that the finches are less likely to fly down when you try to enter the aviary, but crawling through this type of entrance onto a muddy floor when it is pouring with rain will make you doubt the wisdom of such a design, especially if you slip and a bird is able to fly out past you.

A small shelter

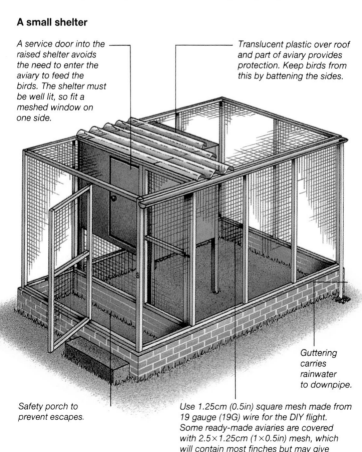

A service door into the raised shelter avoids the need to enter the aviary to feed the birds. The shelter must be well lit, so fit a meshed window on one side.

Translucent plastic over roof and part of aviary provides protection. Keep birds from this by battening the sides.

Guttering carries rainwater to downpipe.

Safety porch to prevent escapes.

Use 1.25cm (0.5in) square mesh made from 19 gauge (19G) wire for the DIY flight. Some ready-made aviaries are covered with 2.5×1.25cm (1×0.5in) mesh, which will contain most finches but may give access to vermin, such as mice.

Large shelters

The most effective option remains the full-size shelter, built on similar lines to a shed. Indeed, you may be able to convert a disused garden shed for this purpose and simply attach the flight to it. A large shed can be used not only as a shelter, but also as a birdroom.

Remember that natural lighting is an important consideration, since the finches will be reluctant to enter a dark structure. Incorporate at least one window into the shelter. If it is accessible to the birds, be sure to cover it with a wire-mesh framework. Otherwise, the birds may attempt to fly through the glass, with fatal consequences. It might be worth installing a double-glazed unit, rather than a single frame of glass, since this will make the aviary more secure. However, in particularly hot climates, you should be able to remove the window so that the temperature within the shelter does not rise excessively during the day.

The dimensions of the entrance into the shelter vary, but a hole measuring about 15cm(6in) square will normally suffice. This is usually located to one side of the door that connects the flight and shelter, or it can be incorporated into the door. If the entry hole is cut to one side of the shelter, it is possible to close the entrance from outside the aviary, thus confining the birds either in the shelter or in the flight.

Position the entrance quite close to the roof of the aviary and at least 15cm(6in) from the edge of the shelter. If you fit runners above and below the entrance hole, you can then set a cover into position that slides across the entrance. Using a wire loop you can pull the cover back and forth over the entrance hole as required. This can be very helpful during periods of bad weather, or if you want to carry out any work in the flight. You may want to take new perches into the aviary, for example, that are too large to fit into the safety porch. In such cases, you would need to open both the inner door and the porch door at the same time, thus offering the birds an escape route.

To provide easy access to and from the shelter, the finches will need a landing platform, ideally made of plywood, located below the level of the bottom runner. A raised edge on three sides of the platform will help to screen the entrance from draughts.

Assembling the aviary

When you come to assemble the component panels on the prepared base, it will be much easier if someone can help you. Run strips of roofing felt on top of the foundations around the perimeter where the wooden frames will be positioned. These strips will act as a damp-proof course. The traditional way of anchoring the aviary framework to the base is to set bolts in the foundations. The frames, with corresponding holes already drilled in them, are then slipped over the protruding bolts and secured with washers and nuts. A modern and more convenient method is to use 'frame-fixers' driven through the framework into the masonry.

If you are using a garden shed as a shelter, join the sides of the flight together before lifting it onto the foundations. You can then fix the entire flight section into place and join it to the front of the shelter. Then lift the roof unit of the flight into its final position.

If the shelter is made up of individual panels, first erect the panel that is common to both flight and shelter. Then assemble the three remaining flight sections and secure them in position. Finally, assemble the remaining shelter panels and hold the roof section of the shelter firmly in place using appropriate bolts. Fill any gaps with a suitable non-toxic sealant. Apply a double layer of heavy duty roofing felt over the entire surface of the roof and secure the felt with short broad-headed nails.

It is a good idea, certainly in warm parts of the world to paint the felt white to reflect the sun's rays and thus help to prevent the felt from splitting prematurely. Batten

The entrance to the shelter

An entrance hole with a sliding cover helps to confine birds in the flight or shelter.

The hole should measure about 15cm (6in) square. If possible, position it to one side of the shelter and quite close to the roof. A sliding cover is held in place by runners top and bottom.

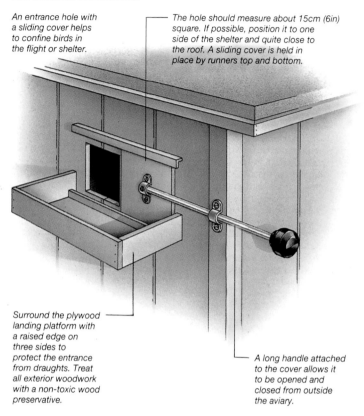

Surround the plywood landing platform with a raised edge on three sides to protect the entrance from draughts. Treat all exterior woodwork with a non-toxic wood preservative.

A long handle attached to the cover allows it to be opened and closed from outside the aviary.

down the loose edges of the roofing felt at the sides so that they will not be blown loose and possibly torn in a storm.

Inside the shelter
When you have assembled the components of the flight and attached them to the shelter, you can put the finishing touches to the interior of the shelter.

Line the inside of the shelter with hardboard and paint this if you wish. Insulation material behind the lining can help to reduce heating costs, especially in a birdroom. A proprietary insulation quilt is ideal for the purpose, but you can use other, cheaper materials, including expanded polystyrene.

The edges of the hardboard should butt up as flush as possible.

This not only looks more attractive, but also makes it more difficult for rodents to gain access to the area behind the lining. These pests can become a major problem if they establish themselves. If they start to breed, their insanitary habits and unpleasant odour may mean that the shelter or birdroom has to be completely relined.

Attach the lining to the framework with panel pins. Careful planning will avoid unnecessary wastage of material; offcuts from the area around the windows, for example, can be incorporated above the entry hole.

Many sheds and most aviary shelters are supplied with a wooden floor. If you build your own structure, however, you may prefer to incorporate a concrete floor, laid on a well-compacted base of hardcore with a layer of thick polythene sheeting as a damp-proof membrane between the hardcore and concrete. Alternatively, you can lay the wooden floor – first treated with a preservative on its lower surface – onto a similar concrete base. A third option is to lay a washable floor covering, such as vinyl flooring, which should prove easier to clean than tiles. This is a particularly good choice for a birdroom, as it is easy to wipe the floor regularly with a damp mop and a solution of disinfectant.

The internal flight

Carefully plan the internal design of the birdroom from the outset, so that you make the best use of the space available. For example, an inside flight – very useful for accommodating young stock or overwintering other birds in heated surroundings – will fit conveniently down one side of the structure. You can build it on the same lines as the outside flight, although the timber framework need only be 2.5cm(1in) square, and obviously will not require weather-proofing.

You can incorporate removable sliding partitions into the internal flight, which fit into runners at the top and bottom of the structure. The gap through which to slide the partition should not exceed 1.25cm (0.5in), so that the finches remain within the flight. If a larger gap is required, use a strip of battening to close the opening. Construct the battening so that it hooks or bolts into place, without the need to unscrew the boarding whenever the partition is moved.

The arrangement of doors in the flight will be influenced to some extent by your decision to include a partition. If there is a partition, then you will need two doors to give access to each part of the flight.

Rather than enter the flight to clean it, you may prefer to construct sliding trays that fit on the floor. Fix a handle at the front to enable you to pull the tray out easily and raise the edges of the tray to prevent seed husks being scattered around outside the flight as the finches fly about their enclosure. If there are to be high edges around the perimeter of the tray, the front of the tray will also need to be raised, so be sure to make due allowance for this height when you construct the front of the flight.

Breeding cages

You will need cages in the birdroom, especially if you want to keep Australian finches, which are traditionally bred in these surroundings in much of Europe and North America. Exhibition breeders of Bengalese finches also use cages so that they can pair their stock selectively and maximize the likelihood of breeding winning birds.

Suitable breeding cages are available from many aviary manufacturers, or you can construct them yourself. The traditional breeding cage is built with a solid base and sides, and affords the birds more seclusion than the traditional open-wire cage popular for pet canaries or budgerigars. Although hardboard is cheaper, it is better to construct the box of thin plywood, which is more durable.

Finches are active birds, so the breeding cage should be relatively spacious. If you decide to build the cage yourself, then you will need to plan it around the size of the cage fronts that you can buy individually in a variety of sizes. Those manufactured for finches have a narrower bar spacing than fronts for budgerigar cages. In most cases, the fronts are 30cm(12in) in height, which allows for the cages to be 35cm(14in) high overall, with space for a sliding tray to fit beneath the front. Individual breeding cages should be at least 45cm(18in) long overall. Again, as with an indoor flight, you can partition the cages so that they form either double or treble units. This increases the flexibility of the cages, so that you can use them for stock-holding or weaning purposes when necessary.

Above: *Tiers of breeding cages in a light and airy birdroom. Position the cages out of draughts and at a convenient height for cleaning.*

It is certainly advisable to cover the interior of the breeding cage with a pale-coloured emulsion paint. Any gaps or crevices within the cage will offer red mites an opportunity to become established, so you may decide to seal these holes with a thin layer of silicone aquarium sealant. Once dried, the sealant is water-resistant, so that even when the cages are washed, the crevices will not become saturated. The finches should ignore the sealant, but may be attracted to any loose strands. Once it has set, the sealant takes on a rubbery feel, and you can simply cut the loose ends with a sharp knife or scissors.

Perches should run across the cage, from back to front. Thin dowelling is popular for this purpose, and two perches are usually included in the breeding cage. Before fixing them in place, check that the finches have enough room to turn round easily, without damaging their tails. The simplest means of securing the perch is to glue it to the back of the cage, and to cut a vertical slit into the front. You can then slot the perch into the

cage front, where it will remain held in place by the horizontal bar. It is vital that the perches are fixed securely, so that the birds can mate without difficulty. The various options for equipping such cages at the onset of the breeding season are considered on page 49.

You can construct a suitable tray for the base of the breeding cage, or use a galvanized steel tray, complete with a lip. These are available from specialist suppliers, or you can get them made up specially. Take care to ensure that this tray fits snugly into the base of the cage, and that any metal edges are safely bent over, so they present no danger to the finches. The galvanized tray is likely to prove more durable than one of plywood construction.

Within the birdroom the breeding cages can be stacked on top of each other, but do not position the bottom tier at ground level. In this position, the birds may be more exposed to draughts and breeding results often tend to be disappointing. It is better, therefore, to mount the cages at least 30cm(12in) off the ground on a solid base. The cages will also be easier to service in this position. Another option is to mount the cages on wheels, so that they can be easily moved for cleaning purposes and without disturbing the birds.

Electricity in the birdroom
It is always a good idea to seek expert advice and help to ensure that the electrical supply to the birdroom is safely installed. The regulations governing outside sources of power vary from one country to another and a professional electrician will be aware of these requirements. It may be possible to fix the cabling in ducting onto a wall. The alternative is to bury the cable in the ground, to a depth of at least 45cm(18in) as a safety precaution. Remember that you may need to include power points for more sophisticated equipment, as well as a simple lighting circuit.

Lighting

It is useful to have a clear idea of the electrical equipment that you intend to include in the birdroom, so you can plan accordingly. A light will be important, and you may prefer to opt for a special fluorescent tube that emits light of a similar wavelength to that of natural sunlight. The advantage of this type of lighting is that it enables the birds to synthesize Vitamin D_3, as they do naturally when exposed to sunlight. This vitamin plays a crucial role in monitoring body stores of calcium and phosphorus – especially during the breeding season – and appropriate lighting can have an important beneficial effect on finches being kept indoors over the winter months. Alternatively, it is possible to provide Vitamin D_3 in a synthetic form, via the finches' food.

Similar lights, covering the natural spectrum, are marketed for use with plants and are available in bulb rather than tube form. They are not always easy to find, but garden centres sometimes stock them in either screw or bayonet fittings. The wattages of these bulbs can be as high as 150W, but a 60-watt bulb should be adequate for most birdrooms. Never use a bulb that exceeds the recommended wattage of the holder, since clearly this can present a fire risk. It is always worth keeping a spare bulb, as you will eventually need a replacement. A dimmer and a time switch are usually included within the circuitry, to switch the lights on and off automatically. In the past, most dimmers were intended for use only with incandescent light bulbs, but several designs now successfully operate fluorescent tubes. Check that you obtain the correct model for your system. Some of the more advanced dimmers can control both incandescent bulbs and fluorescent tubes.

A dimmer, as the name suggests, will slowly reduce the light intensity, so that darkness falls gradually, enabling the birds to return to their perches or nest, as they would do

Inside the birdroom

A dimmer and time switch give control over light intensity and daylength. Ensure that all cabling is safely installed.

An ionizer purifies the air and destroys airborne bacteria.

Breeding cages, at least 30cm (12in) off the ground, with a solid base and sides offer seclusion to Australian and Bengalese finches. Attach nestboxes to the front or sides of the cages.

Electric tubular heaters mounted on the wall provide warm convected air currents.

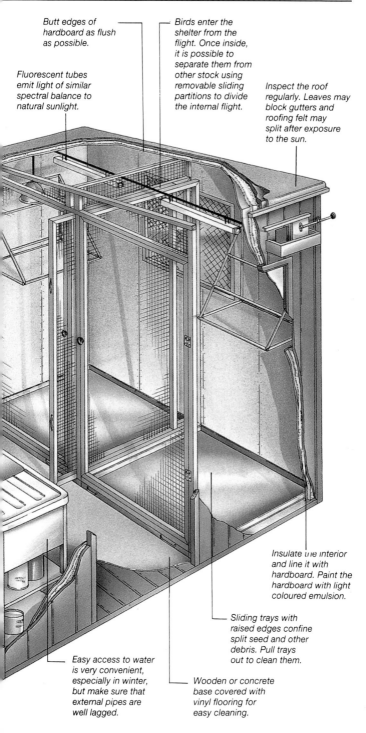

Butt edges of hardboard as flush as possible.

Birds enter the shelter from the flight. Once inside, it is possible to separate them from other stock using removable sliding partitions to divide the internal flight.

Fluorescent tubes emit light of similar spectral balance to natural sunlight.

Inspect the roof regularly. Leaves may block gutters and roofing felt may split after exposure to the sun.

Insulate the interior and line it with hardboard. Paint the hardboard with light coloured emulsion.

Sliding trays with raised edges confine split seed and other debris. Pull trays out to clean them.

Easy access to water is very convenient, especially in winter, but make sure that external pipes are well lagged.

Wooden or concrete base covered with vinyl flooring for easy cleaning.

normally in the wild. In the morning, the process is reversed and the dimmer slowly increases the level of lighting. By this means, it is possible to increase daylength, and provide the finches with a longer feeding period. This is especially valuable on short winter days and enables you to attend to the needs of your birds after dark, without disturbing them.

It is usual to pre-set the dimmer controls, so that they do not need to be altered daily. A more sophisticated system incorporates a photo-electric light sensor, positioned on a window, that detects the light intensity outside. The lights are switched on automatically when the illumination falls below a specific level. On a dull, wet evening, for example, the lights are switched on earlier. This device offers a more flexible and natural means of control than the standard dimmer.

Heating

If the finches are kept in outdoor accommodation during the winter months, it is a good idea to include a heater in the birdroom. Electrical tubular heaters, devised for heating greenhouses, are the safest and most durable option for use in a birdroom. Heat from a central core is liberated via the outer casing of a sealed unit and warms the surrounding air. It is best to mount these heaters on a wall, rather than on the floor, to set up an efficient air flow by convection. Although fan heaters are occasionally used in birdrooms, they are not really suitable, since they soon become clogged with dust.

Tubular heaters are available in various lengths and wattages. The number of heaters required will depend on the area to be heated, the degree of insulation in the structure and the external temperature. Your supplier can advise you about individual requirements. It is preferable to allow for a wattage in excess of your requirements, since this will heat the birdroom more efficiently and, during very bad weather, a more powerful system will be able to cope with the increased demands placed upon it.

Connect the heating unit to a thermostat. This will help to minimize heating costs, and ensure that the temperature does not fall below a level that will cause the finches discomfort. A minimum temperature of 4.4°C(40°F) will be acceptable to birds such as Zebra Finches, but for recently imported finches, the thermostat may have to be set at 15°C(59°F). Bearing this in mind, it could well prove more economical to keep such birds in the home over the winter. By observing the finches carefully, you will be able to recognize if they are uncomfortable. If the temperature is too low, they tend to become less active and perch with their plumage in a ruffled state, looking unhappy in their surroundings.

An infrared lamp can provide an auxiliary means of heating the birdroom. It can be useful for helping to establish recently imported finches, or for treating an ailing individual. You will need a power point to operate such a lamp. Choose a model produced specifically for use with livestock, since this will be more robust and should not break if it is inadvertently sprayed with water. It should emit only heat and not light, since keeping finches in constant light could be disturbing for them over a period of time (See page 58 for details of using a portable unit.)

The unit is usually suspended over an indoor flight with a reflector behind the bulb to direct the warm rays. The finches can then move back and forth, seeking out the warmer area under the lamp's rays if they feel cold. Some infrared units also incorporate a thermostatic setting, so the heat output can be adjusted as required. Various wattage bulbs are available, and the higher wattage outputs produce relatively more heat. The unit itself can be secured quite simply above the flight by means of an inverted clip in the roof; this is adequate to support the weight of the bulb and reflector.

Ventilation

A build-up of dust can rapidly occur in the birdroom and the movements of the birds will keep particles in the air. Good ventilation is important to ensure that the atmosphere remains healthy. You may want to fit an extractor fan to circulate the air, particularly in a larger birdroom. Surround it with a wire-mesh shield, so that if any bird tries to get into the main body of the birdroom, there is no risk of it being sucked into the equipment, with fatal results. If a false wire door is incorporated into the birdroom, it will be possible to leave the main door open when the weather is fine, thus improving ventilation, especially if you can also open the windows within the birdroom or even safely remove them.

However, opening the doors and removing the windows will not be feasible during the cold months of the year, and at these times you should consider using an ionizer. Ionizers are a relatively recent introduction into the field of aviculture, and are still generally available only from specialist outlets or by mail order, but they have been used for a number of years in poultry houses and other agricultural buildings. You do not even need to have an electrical supply to your birdroom in order to use an ionizer here, as some models operate off a car battery.

The cost of using a mains ionizer is negligible, since it uses the same amount of electricity as an ordinary light bulb. The ionizer, in the form of a tube terminating in a needle-like projection, produces a constant stream of electrons. The electrons then collide with molecules in the air and form negative ions that spread out into the room and 'cluster' around airborne particles. Having acquired a negative charge, these particles are precipitated from the air to an earthed surface, such as the floor. Here, the debris can be wiped up with a damp cloth.

Research has shown that an ionizer not only purifies the air by removing dirt, but is also able to destroy airborne bacteria very efficiently. An ionizer can also be useful in an indoor birdroom, where it helps to prevent the spread of dust within the home.

Water in the birdroom

Not many birdrooms incorporate a water supply, but it is well worth including a sink, especially if a large number of breeding birds are accommodated in cages. With a sink close by, you can easily wash pots and other food containers and replenish drinkers without having to make several trips back and forth to the house. Obviously, the feasibility of including a water supply depends to some extent on the locality of the birdroom in relation to the existing domestic supply. Connecting the water supply is probably best undertaken by a plumber. Make sure that the external pipes are well lagged to protect them from freezing in extremely cold weather conditions.

Below: *Ionizers are an ideal way of reducing dust and destroying airborne bacteria in the birdroom. Cheap to run and harmless in use.*

How ionizers work

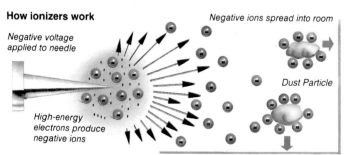

Negative ions spread into room

Negative voltage applied to needle

High-energy electrons produce negative ions

Dust Particle

Earthed surface

As an added extra, a small dishwasher can prove a valuable timesaver, particularly during the breeding season. When installing the electricity supply, bear in mind these extra possible appliances, and fit at least one double socket, even if you do not plan to include a dishwasher. This will give adequate scope to operate other equipment, such as a vacuum cleaner and a winnower, for example. This is a device that separates whole seed from husks so that uneaten seed can be 'recycled' and offered to the birds again.

Aviary landscaping
Having completed the internal construction of the shelter/birdroom, you are now ready to consider the external appearance.

Grass cover
If you did not incorporate a concrete floor or paving stones during the initial site preparation, you can now lay the turves you saved at that time. On the whole, grass cover is more suited to larger enclosures. Do include a gravel path leading through the flight so that you do not damage the grass as you walk through the enclosure. The ground is less likely to become sour, thus allowing moss to replace grass in some parts. Elsewhere, the grass may simply die away. To keep a planted flight with a grass floor looking attractive, provide good drainage and only house a relatively small number of finches in it. Generally, leave the grass to grow naturally, especially when the birds are nesting, but you could use shears to cut it occasionally.

Plants for the aviary
The choice of plants for the outside flight will be influenced by the local climate and the size of the aviary. Some plants are more suitable for larger enclosures, so check on the likely growth rate of the plants you wish to include. This information can usually be found on the plant labels at most garden centres.

Conifers are a worthwhile choice; they grow readily and provide cover throughout the year. They may be used as nesting sites, as will other dense shrubs. Although gorse is popular with many finches it is not usually cultivated in the aviary, probably because of the prickles. However, you can put some pieces of gorse in the aviary at breeding time to provide nesting sites.

Some plants are important because they attract insects into the aviary, which are greedily devoured by many finches when they have chicks in the nest. Waxbills and related species, in particular, tend to breed much better in planted surroundings for this reason. Annual plants are ideal; most of them are easy to cultivate and can provide a colourful scene. Nasturtiums (*Tropaeolum majus*) fit into this category, attracting invertebrates such as black aphids, which are an ideal livefood for rearing chicks. Nasturtiums are available in a range of colours and can be trained up the framework of the flight or allowed to trail over the floor. You can grow runner beans in the same way, and they too will often be colonized by blackfly.

Many finches also appreciate fruiting plants, such as alpine strawberries, which are easy to grow in aviary surroundings. Elder (*Sambucus nigra*) is another useful fruiting plant, but its profuse growing habit may mean that it needs to be cut back regularly. Beware of the damage that some plants can do to an aviary. Russian Vine (*Polygonum baldschuanicum*), for example, will grow very quickly, trailing up the aviary mesh and possibly damaging it by the sheer weight of growth. If only one strand of mesh is torn, small finches may be able to slip through the gap and escape from the aviary.

Once the aviary is completed, it is a good idea to leave the plants for a week or so to establish themselves, before you release the finches into their new quarters.

If you intend to move your finches from the aviary before the onset of the winter, it is worthwhile clearing the plants out at the same time. Discard any annual plants and

Above: *A planted flight attached to a birdroom. The windows adjacent to the door are screened with mesh and open for increased ventilation.*

bring perennials, such as non-hardy fuschias, indoors. In the spring, these plants may benefit from repotting or a partial soil change, so remove the top layer of soil from their container and replace this with fresh compost. A plant food will also prove beneficial. Prune back or divide larger plants at the start of their growing period.

Perches
Unless the aviary includes small trees, such as apple or pear, you will probably need to add some artificial perches. The growing shoots of sycamore are ideal for the purpose, being relatively straight and easy to obtain. Remove the leaves and wash the branches in case they have been soiled by wild birds, which could introduce disease to the aviary occupants. Position the branches lengthways across the flight, and hold them in place with wire looped tightly at either end and attached to the aviary uprights. If you can obtain the crown of a sycamore, you can mount this nearer the aviary floor, set vertically in a large flowerpot.

Do not site the perches above one another, because the lower perches will rapidly become soiled. Ensure that the space beneath the perches is easily accessible, since it is here that the majority of droppings will accumulate, and must be removed. In a flight with a grass floor, it is a good idea to set paving slabs directly beneath the perches for ease of cleaning.

A pond
You may wish to include a small pond in the aviary, but this is not recommended. For one thing, the water will stagnate and could represent a health hazard to the finches. There is also a risk that the birds may drown, unless the water is very shallow. Ideally, provide a shallow propagating tray, available from garden centres, for bathing.

General maintenance
Most aviaries need little maintenance, although regular treatment of the aviary woodwork will help to prolong its lifespan. In the autumn you can thoroughly clean out the entire aviary and expand it, if you wish. At this time of year there is no risk of disturbing breeding birds and you should be able to complete your work before the onset of winter frosts makes construction difficult.

If the floor of the flight is made of concrete or paving slabs, you can thoroughly scrub it with a

33

Above: *A range of inside flights suitable for finches. Indoor accommodation is useful for finches during the colder months.*

disinfectant solution and then wash it over using a hose, if possible. This is much easier than carrying buckets of water from the house into the flight.

Cleaning breeding cages

It is also well worth cleaning out the inside of the birdroom once a year at the end of the breeding period. Dismantle the cages as far as possible and wash them with a disinfectant and acaricide (an anti-parasitic solution) to eliminate not only germs but also mites that may have become established during the breeding period. Carefully discard or burn old nesting material, since this may also contain mites. Such is the viability of these parasites that they are capable of surviving for long periods without food. Red mites can certainly overwinter in breeding cages, increasing rapidly in number once the finches are reintroduced the following year. These parasites can have a particularly debilitating effect on such small birds (see *Health care*, page 61).

Remove all nestboxes and immerse them overnight in a bucket containing the acaricide solution.

This may seem unnecessary if you do not believe that you have red mites in the breeding cages, but it is a valuable precaution. To begin with, these parasites are quite inconspicuous and only when they are well established will they become evident, by which time their effect on the breeding season will be dramatic – even resulting in losses of chicks. At this stage, it will prove much harder and more time-consuming to eliminate them successfully. You may even have to dispose of your breeding cages and replace them with a new set, which is likely to be costly.

It will be much easier to clean the inside of the cages if the cage fronts are removable. Take out the sliding trays and perches and wash them separately. Then, outdoors, use a hose and scrubbing brush to remove any stubborn faecal deposits on the inner sides of the cage. These often accumulate in the immediate vicinity of a nesting pan, and are difficult to remove when the cage is occupied.

When the various components have dried out, you can repaint the interior of the cage if necessary, before reassembling it ready for the following year. It is a good idea to tape plastic sheeting around the front of the cages when they are transferred back to the birdroom. This will protect them over the winter, otherwise they are certain to become dusty and will have to be cleaned again before you introduce the birds in spring.

Cleaning the birdroom

While the birdroom is stripped of cages, you will be able to clean it more thoroughly than usual. Dust and seed husks will probably have accumulated behind the staging where the breeding cages stood, and a robust vacuum cleaner with a sucker attachment will remove this dirt. You can of course sweep it away, but this tends to stir up the dust into the atmosphere rather than remove it.

You can then wash over the floor and redecorate the interior as required. It is certainly best not to have finches in the birdroom, in an inside flight or even in cages while you are painting, just in case the paint fumes are harmful to them. In any event, leave the outer door of the birdroom open, with the wire-mesh frame in place, to dissipate the smell of paint while it is drying.

Before the winter is at its worst, check the roof of the structure. It is better to look for early signs of external damage than to wait until the damp on the birdroom ceiling has discoloured the lining material. Roofing felt may need to be replaced, following exposure to the heat of the summer sun. Make sure that the guttering has not become blocked with leaves or other debris in the autumn, as this could also create further problems during the winter months ahead.

Rats and mice

Rats and mice can pose major problems if they get into the aviary. They will disturb the birds, and are likely to contaminate their food. Rats, especially, may kill finches if they gain access to their quarters. Always suspect their presence if birds disappear from the aviary overnight. A solid concrete floor will help to exclude these pests, however, by making it harder for them to tunnel in underneath the foundations (see page 19). They are most likely to gain access to a large overgrown aviary where the seed is left in the outside flight. In the first place, check carefully around the perimeter for any traces of burrows. These may be sited some distance back from the aviary, concealed in the undergrowth. Remember that excavations within the flight may not be immediately obvious.

Mice tend to be less conspicuous than rats; one of the earliest signs of their presence may be their droppings close to the food pots. The high reproductive rate of these creatures under conditions where food is plentiful means that they must be eliminated without delay. It is obviously dangerous to use poisons in an aviary, and traps can prove equally hazardous. But there are two safe options: a live trap or an ultrasonic rodent scarer.

Live traps

You can place a live trap anywhere within the aviary without fear of harming the finches. Live traps vary in design, but they tend to be made up of two basic components: a box and a roof section, which consists of wire-mesh entry tunnels on a wooden frame. The mice enter the box through the tunnels but are unable to escape. In order to be effective, leave the trap open and baited for several nights. Remove other sources of seed from the aviary, to encourage the mice to feed in the trap and then, once the lid is in place, as many as ten mice can be caught during a single evening. Always eliminate rats without any delay. First, find how they are getting into the aviary and block up these entrances. Then seek the advice of a pest control firm, since they will offer the most effective means of destroying rats.

Ultrasonic rodent scarer

You may decide to fit an ultrasonic rodent scarer in a birdroom, or even in an aviary shelter. This device emits high-pitched sounds that are disturbing to the rodents' nervous system but cause no harm to the birds. Fortunately, it appears that rodents cannot build up an immunity to ultrasonic sound.

Feeding

To describe finches as 'seedeaters' is to reveal only one aspect of their feeding needs. Seeds are deficient in certain vital respects and these deficiencies need to be made good if finches are to have a full and varied diet. For example, seeds tend to be low in certain amino acids, which are individual constituents of proteins. The so-called 'essential' amino acids can be supplemented by feeding livefood. Similarly, seed contains only a low level of various vitamins and minerals.

The seed diet
Finches are not difficult birds to cater for and seed will feature prominently in their diet. The seeds typically included in finch mixtures – sold as British Finch Mixtures or Foreign Finch Mixtures – can be divided into two basic categories: cereal seeds and oil seeds.

Cereal seeds
These contain a relatively high proportion of carbohydrate and usually form the basis of the diet for waxbills and munias. Millets and canary seed are the principal cereal seeds in Foreign Finch mixtures.

Millets vary in their palatability. The small Japanese and panicum millets are more popular than the larger pearl white variety. Panicum millet is also available in a spray form – made up of the seedheads of this particular grass – which is very popular with all finches. Although relatively costly, little seed is wasted when panicum is offered in spray form, whereas loose seed tends to be scattered quite readily.

Below: *A Crimson-rumped or Sundevall's Waxbill* (Estrilda rhodopyga) *feeds on a millet spray, a convenient source of seed.*

Canary seed is the other significant cereal ingredient of a finch mixture. The crop is grown in various parts of the world and, as with millets, it may be worth mixing different types of canary seed together, in order to counteract any deficiencies in the different growing areas. Seed analyses do vary, depending on local growing conditions and the amount of fertilizer used on the crop.

Oil-based seeds

These contain a relatively high level of oil (fat), and are higher in protein than cereal seeds. Although a mixture of cereals forms the basis of the seed diet of many finches, some species – notably members of the family Fringillidae (the 'true' finches) – require a more varied mix that includes oil-based seeds, often sold as a British Finch Mixture. A typical canary mixture is also suitable for these finches. In addition to plain canary seed, this mix contains red rape, a small dark reddish seed. These two seeds are included in approximately equal quantities in such mixtures.

Hemp is one oil seed that may be added to the mixture. This fairly

Above: *Plastic containers which hook over the aviary mesh or cage front are useful as seed pots and for offering softfood to the birds.*

large, brown, circular seed has a relatively high oil content. Traditionally, larger quantities of hemp are offered to birds kept in outside aviaries during the winter because it provides a concentrated source of energy that helps the finches to maintain their body temperature during cold weather.

Do not, however, offer the birds an unlimited supply of hemp. They may become obese if they eat too much of it and it can affect their plumage, creating a condition known as induced melanism. This is known to affect bullfinches and other Eurasian finches that have been fed a diet high in oil seeds over a period of time. The birds moult out, showing abnormal areas of blackish plumage in place of their usual body coloration. If the seed mixture is altered, and the relative proportion of oil seed – notably hemp – is reduced, the plumage should revert to normal at the next moult, but in the interim nothing can be done to alter the bird's coloration.

Niger is another oil seed often included in seed mixes. It has an unmistakable appearance, being thin and black. It is claimed that niger can help to prevent egg-binding, a condition to which certain species of finch tend to be susceptible, but there is no real evidence to support this view.

Blue maw, a small bluish oil seed derived from poppies, is certainly useful during the breeding period, and makes an ideal weaning food for young finches, especially when sprinkled over a softfood.

Unusual seeds
The less common seeds, such as teazle, gold-of-pleasure and white lettuce, are usually obtainable only from specialist suppliers, who advertise in the various birdkeeping publications. You can buy the seeds individually and add them to a seed mix. Alternatively, they often feature in the various 'tonic' or 'condition foods', which are typically used either before the breeding season or when the birds are moulting. These mixes also add valuable variety to the finches' diet throughout the year.

Seed quality
The quality of the seed used in mixtures can vary, and although it is not possible to gain a reliable

impression of the seed's nutritional value just by looking at it, you should examine it carefully. It should be clean, free from dust and run easily through the fingers. Provided it is kept dry and out of reach of rodents, you can store seed satisfactorily for several months. Most mail-order suppliers deliver seed in paper or hessian sacks but, although these are robust, it is safer to store the seed in metal bins.

Soaked seeds
As well as dry seed, many finch breeders offer their birds soaked seeds. These are easy to prepare; simply place a small quantity of dry seed mix in a bowl and cover it with warm water. A day later, pour away the surplus water, restraining the seed in a sieve. Rinse the seed thoroughly and then transfer it to a container for the finches.

This process fulfils two functions; firstly it softens the seed, making it more palatable and digestible for the finches. Soaked seed is especially valuable, therefore, for young or ailing birds that are finding it difficult to crack hard seed. Secondly, it makes a useful addition to the diet, since the germination process started by immersion in water alters the nutritional value of the seed. The protein value is increased, and the

Left and below: *Sprouted seeds have a high nutritional value for finches, especially during the breeding period. Rinse before use.*

accompanying chemical changes improve the vitamin levels.

However, once it has been soaked, the lifespan of the seed as a viable food is strictly limited. Remove uneaten soaked seed after one day, before moulds develop that could harm the birds if they eat the seed. As well as the conventional seeds used as birdfood, you can prepare various pulses, such as mung beans, in a similar way, taking care to wash them thoroughly as before. You can sprout seeds and pulses using one of the kits available for this purpose. The developing shoots, chopped into small pieces, are especially palatable to many finches.

Greenfood

If finches accept them, greenfoods can be a useful food supplement, adding vitamins and minerals to the finches' diet. Otherwise, they are of little nutritional value, consisting largely of water. Wash all greenfood very thoroughly before giving it to the finches and never collect plants from areas where any chemical sprays might have been used regularly. Plants from roadside verges are also unsuitable, since the vegetation here may be heavily contaminated with exhaust fumes. The supply of greenfood will also be influenced by seasonal availability.

Chickweed (*Stellaria media*) is one of the most popular wild plants for birds. It will grow throughout the year in a moist, slightly shaded part of the garden. Spinach beet (*Beta vulgaris*) is a valuable greenfood that can be grown quite easily from seed and harvested throughout the year. Choose a strain that contains a low level of oxalic acid; this could affect the finches' calcium reserves if consumed in quantity over a period of time. The leaves are quite large and, if laid flat, may be difficult for the finches to nibble. If you hang the leaves up by their stalks, they will be more accessible to the birds. You can also use special greenfood racks; these are especially useful for chickweed, ensuring that it does not become covered in seed husks on the feeding table.

The other alternative is to cut up all greenfood into small pieces using a sharp knife. This method is often used at breeding times to ensure that the birds do not incorporate the food into the nest, where it will rapidly wilt and frequently turns mouldy. A versatile plastic container that simply hooks over the aviary mesh or a cage front is useful for chopped greenfood. In the shelter, you can hang it on the mesh covering of the window. If this is not practical, drive a pair of netting staples into the woodwork and hook the container onto them. If there is no feeding table, always try to position containers close to the perches to minimize spillage and attract the finches to the food.

Other fresh foods

Some finches will take sweet apple cut into chunks, and others favour grated carrot. Carrot is a particularly valuable natural colouring agent for certain species, whose colour will fade in captivity over successive moults, unless the necessary carotenoid pigments are available (see page 41).

Softfood

The description 'softfood' is applied to any avian foodstuff of a loose consistency and may have to be mixed with water. Softfoods traditionally help to compensate for deficiencies arising from a diet of seed alone but, unfortunately, not all finches will take them. Domesticated birds, such as the Zebra Finch, are usually willing to accept softfoods, unlike many African waxbills, for example.

Breeding successes are more common with birds that do take softfood, so it is worth making every effort to encourage reluctant individuals to accept this unfamiliar food. However, a significant number of species of finch will eat only insects, spiders and other invertebrates at breeding time, regardless of their relative nutritional value, so strong are their natural instincts.

Livefood

Most finches will greedily consume a variety of livefoods. Specialist suppliers offer livefood in bulk or as starter packs for those wishing to establish their own cultures. Some livefoods are more satisfactory for finches than others.

You do not have to rely entirely on cultured foods, however, since birds in a planted aviary will, of course, forage and catch insects for themselves. But if there is a shortage of livefood, it is unlikely that all the chicks will be reared successfully. You may like to offer wild-caught invertebrates, such as spiders or aphids.

Here we consider a selection of common livefoods that can be included in the finch diet.

Whiteworm is a particularly valuable soft-bodied livefood. These minute threadlike worms are not cultured in commercial quantities, but it is easy to establish a culture in a constant temperature of about 20°C(68°F).

Thoroughly wash an empty margarine container and punch small ventilation holes in the lid. Fill the container quite close to the top with slightly moistened peat. Bury some bread soaked in milk just below the surface of the peat, along with a small cluster of whiteworm.

Replenish the bread at intervals and spray the surface of the peat regularly to prevent it drying out. The whiteworm remain clustered close to their food source, and after about a month you can start harvesting them carefully from the culture. Pick out clumps of the worms with tweezers and place them in a saucer of water to separate the debris from the whiteworm. You can culture other small worms, such as microworms and grindalworms, in this way.

Mealworms, in spite of their name, are not worms, but the larvae of the Meal Beetle (*Tenebrio molitor*). They are the most widely available livefood, but are not entirely suitable for finches, especially during the breeding period, because young chicks find the hard body casing relatively indigestible.

However, mealworms are easy to keep in a plastic tub with ventilation holes punched in the lid. Fill the container with chicken meal and lay small pieces of apple on top to provide the mealworms with moisture. They grow by a series of sequential moults, shedding their hard body casing each time and temporarily taking on a whitish appearance. At this stage, finches with chicks will find the mealworms much easier to digest. Alternatively, you can resort to chopping up mealworms, but this is not a pleasant task.

Crickets are bred commercially in large numbers and are available in various sizes. This livefood, less often given to finches, deserves to be more popular. The hatchlings are tiny and ideal as a rearing food for chicks, but adult crickets can be almost 15mm(0.6in) long. Clearly, invertebrates soon escape if they are simply turned loose in an aviary. If you put them in the fridge for a time before releasing them, however, the low temperature slows down their level of activity sufficiently for the birds to catch them more easily.

Locusts are also available from livefood suppliers, but these tend to be too large for finches.

Fruit flies (*Drosophila*) are another potentially valuable source of livefood. In avicultural circles, fruit flies are best known as a food for hummingbirds that hawk insects in flight. However, there is a variant of the fruit fly that possesses only vestigial wings. Because these flies cannot use their wings effectively, they are particularly valuable as livefood for finches, since they are far less likely to escape when offered to the birds.

Earthworms are too large for many species and must be 'cleaned' before being offered to the birds. Place them in a container of damp grass and keep them in a cool spot for a couple of days or so. During this period, the worms void their intestinal contents and should then be safe for the birds to eat.

Colour feeding

Not all finches require colour food, but birds with red or orange plumage – notably various cardinals and weavers – will certainly benefit from it. All birds exhibited at shows must have the full depth of natural coloration, and colour feeding is essential.

Synthetic colour food is available in various forms. You can administer the liquid form via the bird's drinking water, but be sure to prepare the correct dilution to avoid spoiling the finch's colour by

Below: A colour food will help to maintain the fiery coloration of the beautiful Virginian Cardinal.

providing an excess of the colouring agent. Although this will not harm the bird, it will certainly spoil its appearance. Reddish droppings are an early sign that the finch has been given too much colour food. A softfood mixed with a colouring agent is available in packeted form; give the bird a small quantity of food in the hook-on container provided.

It is not necessary to use the colouring agent throughout the year. The blood supply to the feathers is active only when new feathers are forming and growing, so it is only at the moulting stage that colour feeding will have an effect. In a mixed aviary, it will not matter if birds that do not require colour feeding ingest the colouring agent. The products are very safe and have no serious side effects.

Grit, charcoal and rock salt

Because seed forms the basis of their diet, finches rely on grit to assist in the breakdown of the relatively hard seed kernels in their gizzards. The mineralized grit marketed for budgerigars is suitable for finches and should be constantly available. You can provide grit in tubular containers attached to the cage or aviary, but, check that the flow of grit does not become obstructed.

You can mix mineralized grit with oystershell grit. This dissolves more readily in the gizzard and is a valuable source of minerals. Granulated charcoal is also included in some grits and is worth offering to Australian finches that may include the material in their nests. The reason for such behaviour is unclear, but it may be linked to nest hygiene. Charcoal may help to dry out faecal matter from the chicks and remove any odour, thus helping to conceal the nest from predators in the wild.

Some breeders also provide rock salt for Australian finches. In the wild, some birds have been reported to feed on salt around water holes. The practice of offering rock salt – available from many supermarkets – is most common in mainland Europe and, although it is not essential, there are signs that this practice is becoming more widespread.

Below: *A cuttlefish bone to provide extra calcium, a feeding stick and an iodine block, are positioned within easy reach of the perch.*

Cuttlefish bone

Cuttlefish bone is a valuable source of minerals, especially calcium. It should be made available to all finches throughout the year, although they may only consume it in any quantity during the breeding period. The finches gnaw at the soft powdery side of the bone, and this also helps to prevent their beaks from becoming overgrown. If they find it difficult to peck at the surface, you can cut off chunks with a knife and place these on the feeding tray. Special metal clips are available to attach cuttlefish bones to the aviary or cage mesh.

Nutritional supplements

The most reliable way of providing additional vitamins and minerals for finches is to use a proprietary supplement on a regular basis. Supplements in powdered form will satisfy all the finches' requirements and are easy to administer. Simply sprinkle them over wet greenfood. Do not add the powder to dried seed, since it tends to be lost at the bottom of the container.

Alternatively, you can add a vitamin and mineral solution to the finches' drinking water. Again, it is important to follow the manufacturer's instructions; mix the supplement with water in a measuring jug to avoid overdosing, which can have adverse side effects over a period of time.

Food containers

Various containers are suitable for finch mixtures and here we consider some of the options.

Seed hoppers that hold a generous quantity of seed are particularly useful for feeding finches in cages, since they only need replenishing once a week. Special plastic bases are available that form seed hoppers when a glass jar of seed mix is inverted on top. The birds are thus guaranteed a clean source of seed, since the bulk of the mix is retained within the closed glass jar. Nevertheless, you should check the seed supply every day, since a small obstruction, such as a stone, may impede the free flow of seed.

Plastic containers fitted outside the cage have become more popular for dispensing seed to finches. A broad based container is better than the more conventional tubular design, as the flow of seed is less likely to become blocked.

Glazed pots can be useful in aviary surroundings, where it may be more difficult to find a suitable spot to fit a plastic container. Since they are relatively heavy and not easily tipped over, you can safely place them on a tray on the aviary floor.

A feeding shelf, simply a wooden shelf attached to the side of the shelter with brackets, is an ideal way of supporting feeding containers off the ground. Do not create an elaborate structure where debris can accumulate, and where fodder mites introduced on seed can establish themselves. Ensure that it is broad enough to accommodate the containers comfortably, with space for the finches to fly on and off easily. Ideally, provide separate shelves for moist greenfoods and seeds. This will help to keep the seed dry.

Drinking vessels

Only sealed drinkers are recommended for finches, since the water will remain much cleaner in these containers than in open pots. Use a bottle brush to clean containers thoroughly once or twice a week, and certainly on the day after you have given the birds a food supplement or any form of medication. If you wash the drinkers with detergent, be sure to rinse the containers thoroughly before refilling them.

The volume of water drunk by the finches will vary, depending partly on the temperature of their environment. Water consumption often increases quite noticeably when there are chicks in the nest and at this stage you may need to provide a larger, or even a second drinker. This is particularly

Above: *A seed hopper and tubular drinker complete with attachment clips. Sealed containers are more hygienic, but ensure that the flow of seed does not become blocked.*

important if the birds are left alone for most of the day and there is no-one available to replenish their supply of fluid.

Feeding the finches

The most convenient way of preparing your own feed mix is to add scoops of the different seeds to a carrying container and stir them together. You can then use the scoop to dispense seed mixture to individual cages or flights. You may feel that this is a rather wasteful way of feeding the finches,

especially when you see them empty the food container in search of hemp, for example, and scatter the less favoured seeds in all directions. But to provide the seeds separately is time consuming and, in the confines of a cage, individual containers will take up a disproportionate amount of the available space.

Always feed the birds in the shelter, since here the seed will remain dry and is less likely to attract rodents. If you cover the shelter floor with newspaper, you can use a winnower to reclaim spilt seed, provided it has not been contaminated with droppings or mixed with wet perishable food. There are various designs of winnower and some are more efficient than others. As the seeds and husks fall down within the winnower, an air flow separates out the husks and the seeds fall into a separate container. Over a period of time, you can recoup the cost of a winnower in terms of the whole seed that you recover.

Feeding routine

Finches need daily attention throughout the year, although it is possible to leave them with adequate food and water over a weekend, provided that a friend or neighbour checks each day to see that all is well. (This is always a wise precaution because, as well as ensuring that the birds are fed,

Below: *A Green Singing Finch feeding on seeding grass. In a planted aviary, birds can forage for seeds and invertebrates.*

there will be someone to cope with emergencies, such as a bird becoming caught up by its claws and being unable to free itself. Left unattended, a bird could remain in this position until your return.)

Most birdkeepers attend to their birds morning and evening. During the breeding period, it is useful to feed the finches during the middle of the day as well, to ensure that livefood is constantly available to meet the demands of the growing chicks. If a midday feed is impractical, try to offer less mobile livefood, such as whiteworm rather than, say, small crickets. The finches will then have a readily accessible supply of livefood on which to feed throughout the day. In addition, a well-planted flight will attract insects and spiders, enabling the finches to forage for suitable invertebrates.

Breeding and rearing

During the warmer months of the year, most finches will attempt to breed and some may prove prolific when housed in suitable surroundings. The Zebra Finch will nest readily, but others – notably those whydahs with parasitic breeding habits – present the determined aviculturist with a considerable challenge.

Some finches depend on livefood during the rearing phase and the availability of a suitable diet has a significant influence on the possibility of breeding the birds. Waxbills as a group become highly insectivorous when they have chicks, whereas other finches – notably the so-called munias or mannikins – are far less dependent on livefood for breeding success. Indeed, it is possible to rear the chicks of these birds even if no livefood is provided for the adults. In the second part of the book we discuss the specific feeding requirements of the various groups of birds, along with breeding details of the individual species.

Sexing finches
Some finches are easy to sex, using differences in the plumage of cock and hen as a guide, but a significant number of species show no such variations. However, once they are in breeding condition, it may be possible to sex the birds by

other means. For example, the upper beak of the cock Java Sparrow becomes enlarged at this time, while male munias of many species will start to sing in order to attract potential mates. Occasionally, cock birds – notably some whydahs and weavers – moult into breeding plumage, which is a striking contrast to their much duller, so-called 'eclipse' plumage evident during the rest of the year.

On the whole, it is better to house finches in groups, rather than in individual pairs. Indeed, in the case of mannikins and munias, where there is generally no clear cut sexual dimorphism, the birds breed much more readily in a colony. It is not as vital, therefore, to balance the sex ratios of these birds as it is in the case of birds housed in pairs. For this reason, and also because finches are relatively inexpensive to buy and small in size, finch keepers rarely resort to employing the sexing methods devised for parrots and even softbills.

The size of the aviary will clearly influence the number of birds you can house together. As a guide, a group of eight munias could live quite satisfactorily in a flight about 270cm (9ft) in length, with a shelter attached. Hopefully, with this number of birds, you will have at least two pairs in the colony.

Above: *In some cases, such as the Zebra Finch, recognizing breeding pairs is not difficult. The cock bird is shown here on the right. Most finches will breed in groups.*

Above: *Some cock finches, such as this Combassou, undergo a change in coloration when breeding. (Top) nuptial plumage is black; (centre) eclipse is brown; (bottom) the transition stage is mottled.*

Nest boxes in the aviary

In a planted aviary, a number of natural nesting sites will be available, but it is best to supplement these with a selection of artifical containers in which the birds can choose to build their nests. Some species, such as the singing finches, may adopt a canary nesting pan, constructing a platform-type nest on this base. Most finches prefer more seclusion, however, and may use either a wicker nesting basket or a small nestbox. The basket usually has two strands of wire fitted at the back and these need to be held

Above: *A pair of Gold-breasted Waxbills on their nesting basket. Finches may use artificial nesting sites and build a nest within.*

firmly in place with two netting staples to ensure stability.

The most popular nestbox for finches is the open-fronted design, usually a thin plywood cube, the front of which is left partially open. This affords the birds easy access, but ensures that eggs and chicks will not accidentally fall out of the nest. You can secure the boxes with fixing brackets. Alternatively, fix a longer length of plywood along the back of the box with a strong adhesive and screw the ends to the aviary framework. This is a good way of fixing a number of boxes in a given area. With fewer boxes, it is often better to drill a small hole at a suitable height from the back of the box towards the interior. Then, reversing the process, fix a screw through the hole to a convenient part of the aviary.

Brackets are the best way of supporting closed nestboxes which have a small entrance hole at the front and an access perch beneath. The roof of such a closed nestbox should be hinged to give easy access to the interior. Otherwise, if there is a problem within the nest at any stage, you will not be able to open the box without prising off the lid, which could be dangerous for the occupants. You can buy all these finch nesting receptacles by mail order, although nestboxes are quite easy to build.

Siting the nestbox

The location of the nesting receptacles within the aviary is

Above: *As an alternative to wicker nesting baskets, some finches may prefer small nesting boxes.*

important. Ensure that the finches have an adequate sense of security, so that they will not desert the nest once they have started breeding. Choose a site that is under cover, so that there is no risk of the nest being flooded during a heavy rainstorm. This can cause a fatal chilling of eggs or young chicks, even if the adult birds do not desert the nest.

It may be worth including artificial nesting sites in the aviary shelter, providing the temperature here does not rise excessively during the summer. In an aviary housing a mixed collection of finches, it is a good idea to supply a range of nesting sites located at different heights above ground level, as this may encourage breeding activity.

In the wild, protection from potential predators during the breeding season is obviously important, and this may be why many finches will choose to build a nest in clumps of gorse (*Ulex europaeus*), with its prickly spines. Even if you do not have this plant in your aviary, it is well worth obtaining a number of branches and fixing them in the aviary.

A few finches, including the Quail-finch, will nest on the ground, so the cover provided by a pile of cut conifer branches in a quiet corner of the aviary may encourage a pair to start breeding.

Cage breeding

Obviously, you will have greater control over the birds if they are bred in individual pairs in cages. Maintain an average temperature of 18°C(65°F) in the birdroom and create a day length of 12 hours using artificial illumination. This will enable the finches to breed throughout the year.

There are various ways of fitting nestboxes to breeding cages. They may be attached on the outside, either at one end or on the front. The advantage of fitting nestboxes to the front of the cage is that you can stack up a number of cages in a limited area. Alternatively, you can locate the nestbox inside the cage, but here it will occupy part of the flight that the finches would otherwise use, and in this position it will be difficult to inspect the interior of the nestbox. The same considerations apply to wicker nesting baskets, whether they are fitted to the front or the back of the cage. It can prove especially difficult to remove chicks for banding purposes from baskets suspended in cages, without causing a major disturbance.

Since some species can be nervous when breeding in cage surroundings, a nestbox attached to the side of the cage is probably the best compromise, affording the finches security yet enabling you to watch the progress of their breeding endeavours.

Nesting material

Finches often incorporate a wide range of materials in their nests. Although hay may seem an obvious choice, it is not recommended because it can be heavily contaminated with fungal spores that may harm the birds after a time. Try to avoid materials, such as lengths of cotton, that could become twisted around a toe, cutting off the blood supply and leading to the loss of a digit.

Relatively sterile nesting materials are commercially produced for canaries and these are recommended for other finches as well. Hamster bedding is also suitable as nesting material for birds. Other items include dried moss (available from florists), grasses, and raffia, the latter being especially popular with weavers. As their common name suggests, these finches are inveterate nest builders, the males weaving ornate, pendulous structures that often hang directly from the mesh of the aviary. These attract the females, who team up with a male partner

Below: *Cage breeding is popular for certain species, notably Australian grassfinches. It allows for closer supervision of pairs.*

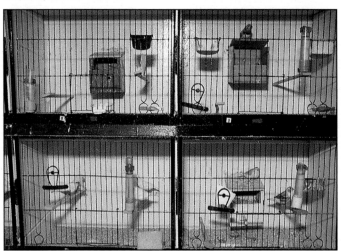

Above: *Weaver finches, such as this Thick-billed Weaver* (Amblyospiza albifrons), *often build ornate nests. Provide suitable nesting material.*

and then help to complete the nest. Unlike most finches, however, cock weavers are polygamous, and build more than one nest, so remember to provide plenty of nesting material if you set up a colony of these birds.

Individual species of Australian finch differ somewhat in their requirements for nesting receptacles. They also show a preference for certain materials with which to build their nests, although all will use dried grass. Provide freshly dried grass rather than hay. Several species of finch are said to favour white feathers when building a nest and you can buy these in a sterilized form from pillow manufacturers. Painted finches, which are terrestrial in their breeding habits, include stones and small twigs in their nests. Some Australian finches use charcoal in their nests and Gouldian finches may use rock salt, presumably because its moisture-absorbing property increases the humidity within the nest.

Birds in cages should be offered small quantities of nesting material each day. This will help to prevent the material from becoming soiled as the birds pull it over the floor of the cage, seeking out suitable lengths. Start with the fibrous materials and then introduce the softer items, which they will use to line the developing structure. In the wild, finches use their beaks to cut off suitable lengths of grass from tussocks. The average length of each piece is about 20cm(8in) and field studies have revealed that the average nest of the Diamond Firetail, for example, consists of about 500 pieces of grass and in excess of 80 feathers. Clearly, breeding birds must have a good selection of nesting material available to them.

Signs of breeding activity

It is easy to see when finches are ready to breed, since, with the exception of weavers, most of these birds show no interest in nesting material or nest building outside the breeding period.

Cock birds will start to display and sing to intended mates. They may become more territorial at this stage, driving off other birds that they perceive as intruders into their area of the aviary. Keep a close watch on the finches during this period to ensure that no bird is unduly harassed by any of its companions. Often, closely related

Below: *A male Red Bishop weaver displaying. A polygamous species, so house a cock with several hens.*

species may start fighting; Cordon Bleu Waxbills, for example, often resent the company of Violet-eared Waxbills. If this happens, you may have to separate the birds to restore harmony within the aviary. The amount of cover available in the flight can also be a significant factor, since, in well-planted surroundings the finches are less likely to come into conflict during the breeding period.

It is often easier to keep a colony of one species of finch that is naturally gregarious and breeds communally, rather than a mixed collection, where individual pairs may disagree with each other.

By careful observation, you should be able to identify the pairs that are building a nest and pinpoint its location. If you do not

Above: *Breeding activity is likely to follow once a cock bird starts to feed an intended mate. These are Alario finches* (Serinus alario).

see one of the birds for several days, especially in a large, densely planted aviary, you may think that it has died or simply escaped. Then, in your subsequent search to check for holes in the mesh, you may inadvertently disturb the sitting bird! Although many finches become tamer when they are breeding, this does not mean that they will stay with a nest when they feel threatened. If possible, do not disturb finches that may be breeding in the outside flight, even if this means a break in the cleaning schedule for a week or so in this part of the aviary.

The risk of egg-binding

There may be few signs, apart from nest-building, that a hen is ready to breed, but be sure to provide an adequate supply of cuttlefish bone in case she needs it. Any shortage of calcium at this stage may be a contributory cause of egg-binding. The calcium deficiency can cause the production of a soft-shelled egg, and may also interfere with the muscular contractions involved in laying it. Eggs with soft rubbery shells, i.e. lacking in calcium, are not easily expelled from the hen's body and create an obstruction.

For some unexplained reason, the condition is relatively common in hen Cut-throats, and may be linked with other deficiencies as well. Any shortage of Vitamin D_3, for example, may also be involved in egg-binding because this vitamin plays a vital regulatory part in the absorption of calcium. Cold, damp weather around the egg-laying period also tends to increase the likelihood of egg-binding.

The signs of egg-binding are quite characteristic. The first indication that all is not well may be when you see the hen away from her nest. She appears very unsteady on her feet and is soon quite unable to perch at all, remaining on the floor of the aviary with her plumage fluffed up. You must take immediate action if she is to make a full recovery. First, prepare a hospital cage (see page 58) and transfer her to it without delay. Maintain the temperature close to 32°C(90°F), and this alone may encourage the hen to lay the egg within a couple of hours or so.

It may be possible to manipulate the egg out of the hen's body, but this is a difficult and stressful procedure for a bird that is already weakened. Be sure to handle a hen suffering from egg-binding with great care, since there is always a risk that the egg could rupture within her body, leading to peritonitis. Working back in a straight line from the vent, you should be able to feel the egg as a swelling. Apply a little olive oil as a lubricant to the vent itself, and then gently massage the egg along as contractions take place. The egg may appear at the vent in due course, but do not undertake such action lightly.

It is better to seek veterinary help if possible. An injection of calcium borogluconate can prove a more effective means of dealing with the problem, and surgery has also been successful in some instances. Nevertheless, the prognosis for a small finch has to be rather guarded, whatever course of action is taken. Birds that do recover should not be used for breeding purposes for several months, to enable them to recover fully.

In aviary surroundings, you can reduce the risk of egg-binding by withholding nesting material and receptacles until the weather is mild. Do not allow the hens to lay excessively, as this obviously depletes their body resources. For this reason, you should restrict hens to three clutches of eggs during a breeding season.

Fostering

The routine practice of transferring the eggs of Australian finches, such as the Gouldian Finch, to pairs of Bengalese is a controversial subject. Some breeders, fearful of imprinting (literally causing chicks to develop an 'identity crisis') are strongly opposed to it. However, without fostering, it is unlikely that the number of Australian finches available today, both in terms of species and individual birds, would be as large as it is.

When Australia imposed a ban on the export of wildlife in 1959, breeding finches took on a greater urgency and birdkeepers with stock started to transfer some of the eggs of their Australian finches to foster parents. This improved the chances of rearing more Australian chicks, since many Bengalese proved to be more diligent parents. Furthermore, when the first round of eggs was taken away, the hen Australian finch would lay another clutch in quite rapid succession and thus increase her reproductive performance.

Above: *Chicks of some species can be transferred to other birds that are more reliable feeders. Here, Gouldian and Bicheno chicks are fostered in a Bengalese nest.*

Do not confuse this type of controlled fostering with a system where Australian finches are *never* permitted to rear their chicks. In such cases, the effects of imprinting are most likely to arise, with the result that the chicks of Australian finches relate more closely to their Bengalese foster parents than to birds of their own kind. Clearly, this will simply compound the likelihood of breeding disappointments in the future, if the fostered Australian finches are then expected to breed naturally.

Under normal circumstances, the risk of imprinting can be decreased quite dramatically by removing the young Australian finches from their foster parents as soon as they are feeding independently. House the Bengalese finches quite separately from the Australian finches. Thus, once the Australian chicks are weaned and back with their own kind, the young birds will no longer see or hear the calls of the Bengalese. In this way, there should be no difficulty when the youngsters are ready to breed.

It can be useful to have several pairs of Bengalese finches in case you need them at breeding time. Not all Bengalese prove ideal foster parents, so it is worthwhile building up a reliable strain. For this purpose, the colour and type of bird are immaterial. Simply select birds from those pairs which have proved most adept at rearing their own chicks and they in turn should make the best foster parents for Australian finches.

Before starting to experiment with fostering, therefore, you should allow the Bengalese themselves to breed, so that you can assess which pairs of birds are likely to be the most suitable for the task. Having established these birds, you can then transfer their own eggs under less reliable pairs when you move the eggs of the Australian finches. Hopefully, the Bengalese offspring will also prove competent feeders in turn.

One of the great advantages of Bengalese is their adaptable natures, as you might expect from a bird which has been developed in captivity and is entirely domesticated. It is possible to transfer the eggs of various Australian finches to one pair of Bengalese. Assuming all the eggs were laid at about the same time, the foster parents will be able to rear the different chicks in one nest without difficulty. This can be especially helpful if an Australian finch hen lays a very small clutch. Rather than allow her to sit on just one egg, for example, it is better to transfer this under a Bengalese, and allow the Australian finch to lay again and, hopefully, produce more eggs in the second round.

In order not to overburden the Bengalese, however, only transfer a maximum of five eggs to each pair, otherwise the resulting chicks may be somewhat stunted, even if they have been fostered by a pair that feed well.

Rearing foods
Well before the eggs are due to hatch, provide the Bengalese with a selection of rearing foods. There are several brands of eggfood that simply need to be mixed with water to a firm, crumbly consistency. Be sure to choose a brand that is readily available, however, since the birds may be reluctant to accept a substitute. Also provide soaked seeds and greenfood, such as chickweed (see pages 38–9). Although livefood is not generally accepted by Bengalese, they may take a softbill food, which will also help in the rearing of the chicks.

Finches in aviary surroundings also need a wide variety of foods, both before and during the breeding period. Perishable foods supplied in the morning should be removed in the evening of the same day before they can sour. Plastic hook-on containers are especially useful for rearing foods; using these you can rotate the pots, placing a fresh supply of rearing food in the aviary when you take away the previous containers.

Fledging and weaning
The finch fledging period is surprisingly short, and the chicks are often out of the nest when just over a fortnight old. The efforts you make during this relatively brief period to supply livefood and other items will be rapidly rewarded when the chicks fledge, but the weaning period is not without its difficulties.

Above: *Young Bengalese or Society Finch chicks soon after hatching. The adult birds will often remove the empty egg shells.*

Above: *As the chicks grow, so the regular supply of rearing food becomes essential. Make up a fresh mixture twice a day if possible.*

Above: *These Bengalese will soon be fledging. At that stage, they are fed by the cock and usually return to roost in the nest at night.*

The cock bird will probably have taken over much of the task of feeding the offspring, since they will not be entirely independent as soon as they leave the nest. At this stage it is important that the young birds are able to find food for themselves quite rapidly, bearing in mind that they may fledge before they are fully able to fly. Under these circumstances, you may decide to offer a selection of foods on the floor of the flight, since the youngsters may be reluctant to enter the shelter.

Put the food in heavy ceramic containers that cannot easily be tipped over. It will not be difficult to keep the flight clean if the pots are placed on a tray or on a clear area of the floor. Be sure to continue offering softfoods and soaked seed to recently fledged finches, since they may be unable to cope with hard dry seed.

If possible, allow weaning to take place gradually and only separate the chicks from the adults once you are sure that they are able to feed on their own. Under aviary conditions, it may be possible to leave the first-round youngsters with their parents for a longer period, providing they do not attempt to interfere when the adult birds nest again. Cage-bred youngsters are usually removed to separate accommodation at an earlier stage, because in a confined space they will almost certainly interfere with the continued breeding attempts of their parents.

A loss of birds during the post-weaning period is not uncommon; Gouldian finches, in particular, may suffer relatively high losses at this time, for reasons which are not yet fully understood. Weight loss, described as 'going light', is often a characteristic feature and in some cases it may simply be that the young finches are removed from the adults before they are able to feed themselves.

On the other hand, 'going light' may be caused by a protozoal infection and good hygiene is vital to ensure that young finches do not succumb to any intestinal disorders (see page 60). When you remove perishable foods, be sure to change the newspaper or other floor lining at the base of the cage. Do not forget to provide a readily accessible supply of grit and cuttlefish bone in these early stages. Once it is clear that the birds are feeding well – usually a fortnight or so after weaning begins – you can transfer them to a flight,

where they can complete their development and strengthen their wing muscles.

Remember that, until now, cage-bred finches will have spent the whole of their lives indoors. It is a good idea to give them an occasional light spray with a plant sprayer to ensure that their plumage is reasonably waterproof before they are transferred to an outdoor flight. Only move them when the weather is fine, and choose a time when you will be available – a weekend, for example – so you can watch the finches carefully and ensure that they settle down without any major problems in their new surroundings.

Ringing finches

Depending upon the legislation in the country concerned, you may be obliged to ring chicks in the nest with a closed circular band that provides a guarantee of the bird's year of hatching in captivity. In addition to this information, the ring may carry a sequential number, the breeder's initials and club details. In the UK, for example, you must ring any native finches that are to be sold for any reason at a later date, and similar restrictions apply in Australia.

Before releasing any birds into the aviary you may want to ring

Below: *Ringing can be useful in identifying birds, but recent research suggests the colour band may affect their status in a group.*

them so you can identify a particular pair or an individual purchase. Split celluloid rings, numbered sequentially, are ideal for this purpose. Unlike closed rings, which are only fitted to young nestlings, split rings are put in place once the bird has fledged. Bands are available in different sizes, so be sure to buy a ring that, once opened and fitted around the bird's leg, can still slide freely up and down. A tight-fitting ring may cause the leg to swell up and may ultimately impair the blood supply to the foot. Keep a watch for any problems, especially in older birds, since their legs tend to become thicker and more heavily scaled.

Celluloid rings are available in a wide choice of colours. In the case of species that cannot be sexed visually, you could choose blue to indicate known cock birds and pink for hens. This information may be useful in a mixed aviary housing Bengalese finches, for example. You cannot read the numbers on the rings from a distance, however, so it is usual to record them, with details such as the bird's origins, in a separate stock register. During the breeding season, you can incorporate some of this information into the breeding register.

Reviewing stock

In late autumn, and certainly if you are contemplating bringing the finches indoors for the winter, you may want to review your stock. Surplus birds can be advertised for sale, or possibly exchanged for seed and other essentials at your local pet store. The exhibition breeder will have had to make a choice of the birds to feature in the show team, but mismarked individuals will appeal to other enthusiasts seeking stock for their garden aviary. Do not exhibit good birds too often, however, since this may compromise their breeding activities later. In most cases, 'current-year-bred' finches should be mature enough to breed during the following season, especially if they were hatched early in the year.

Colour inheritance

A variety of colour mutations has arisen in a number of finches, especially the domesticated species, such as the Zebra Finch and the Bengalese. There are also crested forms of both these species. While some mutations have remained very scarce, such as the Lutino (yellow) form of the Gouldian Finch, others have become very common and are widely available.

A mutation occurs when there is an alteration to the genes – the biological 'code' for all characteristics of the organism, including colour. In most cases, certainly in the wild, any mutant bird is likely to be at a disadvantage, perhaps because a change of colour makes it more conspicuous to predators. There is, therefore, far less possibility that an individual bird will survive long enough to breed and pass on its mutated genes to the next generation. The incidence of mutant genes can be quite high, but it is not always apparent that a bird possesses a gene of this type, since most mutations are said to be 'recessive' to the normal variety. Genes occur on paired chromosomes within the cell nucleus; at its simplest level, genes are paired and only when two recessive genes occur together will a bird appear physically different.

It is no coincidence that mutations are most commonly seen in Australian finches and Bengalese. These birds have been bred in aviary surroundings over countless generations, and stock has therefore tended to become rather closely related. When a number of individuals within a given population carry a mutant gene in their genetic make-up – or genotype – then there is a greater likelihood of the characteristic becoming expressed in a visual – or phenotypic – way. During the mating process, the offspring gain one set of chromosomes (and genes) from each parent. If two birds are closely related, there is a greater chance that each will possess a set of mutated genes and will therefore produce a mutated youngster.

During the last century, scientists began to take a close interest in how various characteristics were passed from generation to generation. The Austrian monk, Gregor Mendel, is best known as a pioneer in this field, analyzing the results that he obtained while working, initially, with pea plants. His findings were to form the basis of the rules of inheritance, which are now widely accepted as providing a means of predicting the likely offspring to emerge from a particular pairing.

Top, right and below: These new mutations of the popular Zebra Finch are most common in Europe at present. They are the Black-breasted (top), the Phaeo (right) and the Orange-breasted (bottom). It takes time to establish new mutations, and the prices of such birds are inevitably high. As more stock becomes available, however, prices fall and official show standards are drawn up for the birds. The majority of mutations to date have been reported in Australian finches.

Health care

Finches can be difficult birds to treat if they fall ill, because of their small size. However, prompt antibiotic treatment as soon as signs of illness are apparent may lead to a spectacular recovery in some cases. Obviously, new acquisitions are more likely to fall ill than established stock, so keep them apart for a period (as described on page 14).

The moult can be another debilitating time, especially for older finches. There will be clear signs of moulting, as the birds drop wing, tail and body feathers in their living quarters. New feathers may appear as spikes, notably on the forehead. Normally the casing surrounding the curled feather is rubbed off or preened away. A food supplement will hasten the finches through this debilitating phase, but it is at this time of the year that losses are most likely to occur so keep a careful check on stock.

Nursing

A sick finch will huddle on its perch with its feathers ruffled. Sometimes the vent plumage is stained and this may indicate a digestive disturbance. A wasting away of flesh over the breastbone and other signs of weight loss are almost certain to be evident as well.

In view of their relatively small size, finches must have warmth if they are to recover. You can buy specially designed hospital cages for these birds, fitted with a heat source and a thermostatic control, which is an essential feature. Such cages will enable you to maintain the temperature at a high level – around 32°C(90°F) – to assist in the treatment process. Then, during the recovery phase – which will take perhaps a fortnight – you should reduce the heat gradually. Avoid returning a finch to its companions in an aviary when the weather is unfavourable.

The hospital cage

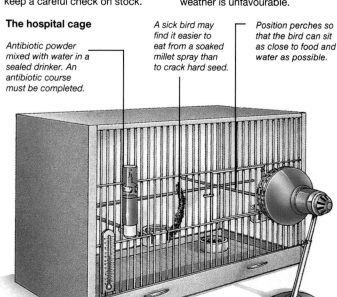

Antibiotic powder mixed with water in a sealed drinker. An antibiotic course must be completed.

A sick bird may find it easier to eat from a soaked millet spray than to crack hard seed.

Position perches so that the bird can sit as close to food and water as possible.

Fit a thermometer to monitor the temperature in the cage. Warmth is essential for small finches when they are sick. Provide a stable temperature of about 32°C (90°F).

Place an infrared lamp close to the cage. The bird can regulate its own position in relation to the heat source.

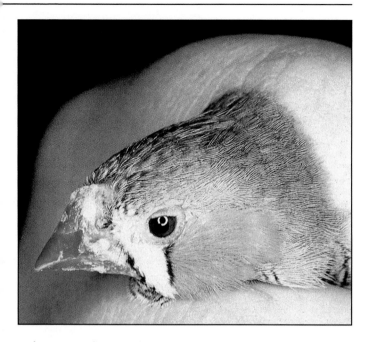

A more versatile alternative to the hospital cage is the infrared heat lamp (see page 30). Instead of heating the environment and then maintaining the temperature at a relatively constant level, you can establish a thermal gradient so that the bird can move closer to the heat source when it needs to.

Your veterinarian will be able to supply the necessary treatment for a sick finch. This may take the form of an antibiotic powder that you mix with water as directed. Do not exceed the recommended dose, since this is likely to have harmful effects. Even if the finch shows signs of recovery, do not stop the treatment until the course of antibiotics has been completed, since this can be equally disastrous. It is obviously important to encourage the bird to drink as much of the medication as possible, so withhold greenfood and do not offer other sources of drinking water. While it is ill, the finch may be more willing to drink from a very small hook-on container or a closed drinker fixed as close to the perch as possible.

The finch may not feel able to

Above: *Scaly face, caused by a mite infestation, is relatively uncommon in finches. Treat it with a proprietary remedy available from a pet store. Isolate affected birds.*

crack hard seed, but a soaked millet spray will often be an encouragement to continue eating (see *Feeding,* page 38). Secure it with a peg within easy reach of the perch. It is also a good idea to extend the period of light, so that the finch can see to feed throughout the entire day. A low-wattage bulb will provide adequate illumination during the night.

Essential hygiene
You cannot rely on medication alone to effect a lasting cure. As well as treating a sick bird, you must thoroughly clean its quarters so that there is no risk of reinfection. Pay particular attention to the feeding area, where droppings could have contaminated seed pots and other containers. Wash all food containers very thoroughly. If you are using a feeding table, line it each day with a fresh sheet of

newspaper folded across and secured to the sides of the table with adhesive tape.

Digestive ailments

To diagnose avian ailments accurately, you may require the help of a veterinarian and the backup services of a laboratory. Detailed analyses can certainly prove worthwhile when a number of birds are affected. For example, it is difficult to unravel the various possible causes of digestive ailments if tests are not carried out. Here we look at two possible causes of digestive problems.

Salmonellosis usually causes quite heavy losses in finches. Dirty surroundings, sour eggfood and contaminated greenfood can all lead to digestive disturbances. Rodents can introduce *Salmonella* bacteria into an aviary, which is just one reason for excluding these pests from the birds' quarters. Greenish, bloodstained diarrhoea is often a symptom of salmonellosis. Take care when handling affected individuals because this bacterial infection may be transmitted to humans. Always wash your hands thoroughly after handling a sick bird in case the bacteria are present on them. They could infect you, especially if you touch food without first washing.

Digestive tract protozoa may cause other infectious problems and can only be accurately identified in the laboratory. In some cases, the protozoa (single-celled parasites) may be carried by the finches and not be the cause of any disease. Typical signs of a more serious protozoal infection of this kind are persistent diarrhoea, coupled with weight loss over a period of time. Affected birds first appear slightly duller than normal and soon develop ruffled plumage. Infections of this type are, in fact, one cause of the 'going light' syndrome. Recent research into this problem has suggested that *Lankesterella*, a blood-borne protozoan isolated from affected birds and usually spread by biting insects, might be transmitted directly via droppings, so good

hygiene should help to prevent transmission of the disease.

Treatment is often possible, using sulpha-based drugs administered via the drinking water for a set period of time. Overdosing finches with these drugs can result in serious toxic reactions, however, so precise treatment is important. Seek veterinary advice.

Feather problems

Finches are far less susceptible than parrots to the vice of feather plucking, but overcrowding or a shortage of suitable nesting material may give rise to this problem. Providing the birds' environmental conditions are improved, the situation should resolve itself in due course, as new feathers grow back uneventfully.

If you see finches preening excessively and their plumage

Below left: Feather-plucking in a Red Avadavat. Compare this bird with the individual shown below. Birds usually recover when offered sufficient nesting material and a less crowded environment.

appears frayed, you may suspect the presence of red mites. These external parasites feed on the bird's blood – hence their common name. Red mites are said to live not on the birds themselves, but rather in their environment and can be transmitted from wild birds. They will cause anaemia – and even death – if present in large numbers. They may be visible as dark specks around the sides and top of the nestbox, where they proliferate.

As a routine precaution, treat all new birds with an aerosol preparation sold specifically to treat mite infestations. Repeat the treatment before the finches are released to join their new companions. This will ensure that all stages in the life cycle have been destroyed. It is also worthwhile treating pairs as soon as they are introduced to the breeding cages. Provided these parasites are not allowed to become established, they are not difficult to control using the preparations described and by keeping the birds' quarters as clean as possible (see *General maintenance*, page 33.)

Breathing difficulties

Not all mites occur on the surface of a bird's body; the so-called 'air-sac mites' localize within the respiratory system of finches. The infection is not confined to Gouldian finches, although they seem to be the most susceptible to it. It is believed that the mites are spread from one generation to the next by adult birds feeding their chicks. The effects of these parasites vary; they may cause mild breathing difficulties or, in severe cases, birds may die as a result of respiratory failure.

Generally, the best time to detect their presence is after dark, when the finches' surroundings are quiet. You may hear a bird breathing rather noisily and notice that its beak is slightly open. This is often a strong indication of air-sac mites, especially if the bird in question appears healthy in other respects. An interesting observation is that affected birds may also show loss of feathers from around the ears, revealing the aural openings which are normally hidden.

Treatment is difficult, although a new group of compounds, known as avermectins, offer the best hope of overcoming these parasites. At present, however, the only way to adminster them is by injection. Some breeders hang dichlorvos strips near the cage of affected finches in the birdroom, but in a confined air space the vapour given off by the strips can be harmful to the birds. The traditional direct method of treatment is to place the finch in a small cardboard box and puff in malathion powder for perhaps ten minutes. The idea is that the bird inhales the malathion into its airways and this kills the mites. Generally, this treatment will have to be repeated over the course of several weeks.

If a number of breeding birds are affected, there is a very good case for allowing their eggs to be fostered to Bengalese. The foster parents will be free of infection and cannot transmit the mites to the chicks, thus breaking the transmission cycle.

A number of other infectious causes can underlie breathing difficulties in finches. You must take even more care than usual when handling affected birds so as not to stress them further. Again, seek veterinary help for an accurate diagnosis of the problem.

Eye infections

A localized eye infection may result from a finch rubbing its head on a dirty perch. In a typical case, the eye appears closed and possibly swollen. There may be a discharge onto the plumage surrounding the eye. If an affected finch is living in an aviary, it will be easier to treat if it is caught and transferred to a cage. An ophthalmic ointment or drops are available from your veterinarian. Applying these several times a day, usually brings about a very rapid improvement in the condition, but you must continue the treatment over a longer period to be sure of resolving the problem.

Although ointment stains the feathers, it is sometimes easier to use than drops, simply because you can be sure that it has reached the required site. When you try to apply drops, a bird may blink, scattering the drop before it enters the eye. It is worth holding the finch for a few seconds after applying the

Below: *Eye infections may result from dirty surroundings. They can often be cured successfully using an antibiotic ophthalmic ointment.*

Above: *A White-headed Nun with overgrown claws. Use bone clippers to trim claws carefully, and do not cut them too short.*

ointment, so that the medication can start to dissolve into the eye, rather than risk it being wiped off straight away onto a perch.

Claw clipping
Many finches will not need to have their claws cut regularly. However, in certain groups of finches – notably weavers, munias and mannikins – the claws tend to grow quickly and, if not trimmed, may cause a bird to become caught up in the aviary.

Use a stout pair of clippers for this task; scissors tend to split the nail, rather than cut cleanly through it. Always check the claws of finches before releasing them into the aviary, as it is easier to clip any excessive growth back at this stage. In finches with pale claws, it is easy to see the blood supply as a thin red streak that stops short of the end of the claw. Cut a short distance away from this so that there will be no bleeding.

If you inadvertently clip too close, dab the end of the claw with a styptic pencil, which should stop any bleeding. The risk of this happening is much greater in finches with darker claws. Even in good light, the outline of the blood vessels is not always clear, so err on the side of caution and snip away just a little.

Species section

In Part Two, we examine individual species of finches and their colour mutations, where these exist. The birds are divided here into five families: the Fringillidae – the true finches; the Estrildidae – waxbills, munias and mannikins; the Viduinae – parasitic whydahs and weavers; the Ploceidae – weavers and sparrows; the Emberizidae – buntings and their allies. We also consider the specific feeding requirements of the various groups of birds and the breeding details of individual species.

There is considerable scope for specialization when keeping finches and you may consider exhibiting your birds in a local show. Exhibition birds are usually bred in cages to guarantee the parentage of the young. Some birds are judged for type (physical appearance) and colour, and points are awarded for the specific features listed in the official standards for the variety concerned. Others are assessed on the basis of their overall condition.

The entries are 'benched' in special cages. These should be in immaculate condition, since the state of the show cage can be a determining factor between two birds of similar merit.

Finches are sometimes exhibited in pairs; where it is possible to sex the species visually, the pair must consist of a cock and a hen. A pair of finches will always win over a single individual of equal merit, simply because it is harder to stage two birds in top condition. Do not be tempted to show a pair of finches together if one is in relatively poor feather, since this will spoil the chances of its companion. Visiting a show, even if you are not exhibiting, is a good opportunity to view many different species of finch and consider them for your own collection. However, before you acquire any new birds, be sure that there is sufficient space in the aviary and that the chosen species will not prove aggressive towards the existing occupants.

Family: FRINGILLIDAE – True Finches
These birds show the typical characteristics of finches as seed-eating birds, possessing stout yet small beaks for cracking seeds. Most species can be sexed by visual means.

Green Singing Finch
Serinus mozambicus

● **Distribution:** Africa, from the Sahara southwards.
● **Size:** 12.5cm(5in).
● **Diet:** A canary seed mixture, with regular supplies of greenstuff.
● **Sexing:** Hens tend to be duller overall, with darker spots on the neck.
● **Compatibility:** Cock birds may be aggressive towards each other, but not towards other birds. House only one pair in an aviary.

These attractive talented songsters are related to the Wild Canary (*S. canarius*). They can be housed quite satisfactorily in a mixed collection and prove relatively hardy and long-lived once established in their quarters. Ensure that pairs have adequate space around their nesting site, so that other aviary occupants do not constantly challenge their territorial instincts.

Below: **Green Singing Finch**
Identical in its requirements to its duller grey relative. These birds can live well over ten years.

Above: **Grey Singing Finch**
This talented songster is often keen to breed, even in a cage. Breeding pairs are best kept apart.

Grey Singing Finch
Serinus leucopygius

● **Distribution:** Ranges across much of northern Africa from Sudan and Ethiopia.
● **Size:** 10cm(4in).
● **Diet:** Typical canary seed mixture, including smaller oil seeds such as maw. Will also take millets.
● **Sexing:** No visual distinction possible.
● **Compatibility:** Keep recognized pairs apart.

Compared with the Green Singing Finch, this is a relatively dull species. You can recognize immature Grey Singing Finches by the pronounced streaking on their breasts. However, the Grey Singing Finch is popularly regarded as a better songster and, during the breeding period, the song of the cock bird is most noticeable. Successful cage breedings have been recorded; a pair will usually attempt to nest using a plastic canary nesting pan or a partially open nestbox. At this stage, you should offer the birds a suitable rearing food and livefood so that when the eggs hatch, there should be no difficulty in rearing the chicks. The hen will lay a clutch of up to four eggs and the incubation period averages two weeks, depending on when the hen started to sit in earnest. After about a fortnight the chicks leave the nest and the adult birds may start breeding again, selecting a new site for this purpose.

Other related species occasionally available include the Giant Green Singing Finch, or St. Helena Seedeater (*S. flaviventris*), and the Yellow-rumped Serin (*S. atrogularis*).

Greenfinch
Carduelis chloris

● **Distribution:** Ranges across much of Europe, from Ireland to the Ural Mountains of Russia, and extending into Asia.
● **Size:** 15cm(6in).
● **Diet:** A mixed diet of seeds, including limited amounts of sunflower seed and peanuts. Will also take greenfood and berries when available.
● **Sexing:** Hens are generally duller overall.
● **Compatibility:** Do not mix with smaller finches.

These attractive finches, like other birds found in Europe, are quite hardy during the winter months in temperate climates and can live out of doors throughout the year. They are justifiably popular aviary occupants and nest freely; some colour mutations having arisen in captive stock. The most striking is undoubtedly the Lutino, but such birds are scarce.

The major problem associated with keeping greenfinches is the relatively high incidence of 'going light' that may be encountered in some collections. Affected birds first appear slightly duller than normal, and soon develop ruffled plumage and the characteristic signs of weight loss (see page 60).

Below: **Greenfinch**
Hardy shrubs and conifers are ideal in an aviary housing greenfinches.

European Goldfinch

Carduelis carduelis

● **Distribution:** Found over much of Europe, extending eastwards into Asia and south to northern Africa.

● **Size:** 12.5cm(5in).

● **Diet:** A British finch mix, or a canary seed mix, supplemented with greenfood and livefood.

● **Sexing:** Hens may be duller overall, but this is not a reliable guide.

● **Compatibility:** Usually kept in single species aviaries. Agree well in groups and in pairs.

The European Goldfinch is a very colourful bird and breeders have aimed to improve coloration as far as possible by selectively pairing birds for this feature. Pairs will nest quite readily; in planted aviary surroundings, secluded nesting baskets are ideal for this purpose. European Goldfinches may lay up to seven eggs and these should start to hatch after 13 days. Teazle is a very popular rearing food for these finches; although it can be difficult to gather wild, this seed is available from specialist suppliers. It is also well worth including dandelions in a planted aviary for goldfinches, since the birds delight in eating the ripe seedheads.

Below: **European Goldfinch**
These attractive finches are hardy, and pairs will usually attempt to nest in aviary surroundings.

Assuming all goes well, the young goldfinches should fledge after about a fortnight and the adults may then start nesting again. A regular supply of livefood throughout the breeding period increases the likelihood of raising chicks successfully.

As in the case of the Greenfinch, various distinctive races, other than the European form of the Goldfinch are sometimes available to aviculturists. The Himalayan Goldfinch (*C.c. caniceps*) is a typical example; the Asian forms usually having greyish rather than black head markings.

Common Bullfinch
Pyrrhula pyrrhula

● **Distribution:** Across Europe.
● **Size:** Up to 19cm(7.5in).
● **Diet:** A canary seed mixture with some sunflower seed.
● **Sexing:** Hens are significantly browner overall, noticeably on their underparts.
● **Compatibility:** Tend to be territorial; keep pairs apart.

Again, there are distinctive variations in the appearance of bullfinches from different parts of their extensive range. The Siberian race (*P.p. pyrrhula*) tends to be brighter and larger than other forms, but the true Siberian Bullfinch (*P.p. cineracea*) is a much duller bird, lacking the typical red markings, which are replaced by grey plumage.

In the wild, bullfinches can inflict considerable damage on the growing shoots of fruit crops and in some areas the species has been heavily persecuted. Similarly, these birds may impede the growth of shrubs in a planted aviary. Provide a variety of fruits, berries and twigs with buds when available.

Bullfinches will certainly take livefood when breeding, but will still be able to rear chicks successfully with only a limited supply available. Many pairs with youngsters will take softfoods and other items, such as soaked seed.

Above: **Common Bullfinch**
These finches can be destructive towards growing plants in their aviary, especially in early spring.

Teazle is especially popular at this stage. Colour feeding and natural foods, such as rowan berries, can help to maintain the reddish coloration of bullfinches. Distinguish young cocks by their bluish grey backs on fledging.

Bullfinches, like other European finches, have been used in conjunction with domestic canaries to produce hybrid offspring known as mules. These birds combine the attractive appearance of their European finch parent with the singing prowess of the canary. They are popular exhibition subjects, and can make good pets, but they will prove sterile if used for breeding. Bullfinch mules are produced by pairing a male canary with a female bullfinch. This is the reverse of the normal pairing used. Breeders generally pair a cock finch with a hen canary; since canaries are domesticated, hen canaries are more docile by nature than hen finches and more suitable for cage breeding. The male offspring prove the better songsters.

69

Common Hawfinch
Coccothraustes coccothraustes

● **Distribution:** Europe, extending into western Asia.
● **Size:** 20cm(8in).
● **Diet:** A canary seed mix, supplemented with sunflower seeds and small pine nuts.
● **Sexing:** Hens are duller and brownish overall.
● **Compatibility:** These birds have powerful beaks and can be aggressive when breeding, so keep pairs on their own.

These finches are likely to prove long-lived, especially in aviary surroundings. Cocks may breed successfully for over a decade and can live well into their late teens. A nesting basket containing some short lengths of twig, hung in a secluded part of the aviary may encourage a pair to start breeding. The male builds a platform-type nest, relying heavily on twigs to form the basic structure, and the

Above: **Common Hawfinch**
Hawfinches have powerful beaks, and can inflict a painful bite.

hen lays an average clutch of five eggs. She alone incubates the eggs for about two weeks and the chicks fledge after a similar interval. Livefood is taken greedily when the youngsters are being reared, and dandelion seedheads are also readily accepted.

Other hawfinches from Asia are occasionally available. The large, so-called Japanese Hawfinch (*C. personatus*), which also occurs in China, exceeds 25cm(10in) in overall size. Its beak is correspondingly powerful, so handle this bird with respect. Eastern hawfinches generally have more black plumage on their heads than the European race.

The head of the Chinese Hawfinch (*C. migratoria*) is totally black and this form is smaller than the Japanese. It is sometimes seen in collections.

Family: ESTRILDIDAE – Waxbills, Munias and Mannikins
These are all quite small birds, which are similar in appearance although not in colour. They tend to be highly social by nature and usually can be kept together in groups.

Grey-headed Olive-back
Nesocharis capistrata

● **Distribution:** Ranges across tropical Africa, from Gambia to west Uganda and the southernmost part of Sudan.
● **Size:** 14cm(5.5in).
● **Diet:** Foreign finch mix, especially small millets; invertebrates, notably aphids. May also sample fruit and greenstuff.
● **Sexing:** No visual distinction possible.
● **Compatibility:** Lives sociably in small groups.

Very little is known about this group of waxbills, but three species of Olive-back are recognized. They tend to be very scarce in aviculture, but a few specimens have recently become available and in time, these may provide us with more information about this interesting genus of waxbills.

Some reports suggest that in the wild the birds favour a highly insectivorous diet, and you should certainly offer captive stock as wide a range of livefoods as possible. Aphids and small spiders are said to be popular, but doubtless small crickets would also be quite acceptable. The jaunty, agile movements of Olive-backs are rather reminiscent of tits. Only one nest of these waxbills has been reported; it was made of dried weeds with some grass stems and measured about 18cm(7in) in overall height.

Another group with a similar distribution are the Negro Finches (*Nigrita* species). Again, these birds are not well documented, and equally unusual in avicultural collections at present.

Below: **Grey-headed Olive-back**
This rare avicultural subject is said to be highly insectivorous in its feeding habits in the wild.

71

Aurora Finch
Pytilia phoenicoptera

● **Distribution:** Semi-arid parts of northern Africa, extending eastwards from Gambia to Sudan and Uganda.
● **Size:** 11.5cm(4.5in).
● **Diet:** Foreign finch mix plus spray millet, with greenfood and invertebrates.
● **Sexing:** Hens are duller than cocks, being brownish overall.
● **Compatibility:** Generally safe to include in a mixed collection, but some cocks become aggressive when breeding.

This pytilia is known under various common names, and may be advertised as either the Aurora Finch or Red-winged Pytilia. Although not as common as some waxbills, these birds make attractive aviary occupants. Following a period of careful acclimatization, they can prove quite prolific; a single pair may rear more than ten chicks during the course of a breeding season. Aurora Finches usually choose covered wicker nesting baskets, but may also be tempted to build their nest in a clump of gorse. Both partners share the task of collecting nesting material.

An average clutch may consist of five eggs or more and the incubation period is about 13 days. Suitable livefood is vital for the successful rearing of chicks. The young finches fledge at about three

Above: **Aurora Finch**
This attractive finch is sometimes known as the Red-winged Pytilia.

weeks old and should be fully independent after a further fortnight. If possible, remove them from the aviary before the adults start nesting again.

Melba Finch
Pytilia melba

● **Distribution:** Occurs in a band across tropical Africa, extending across much of southern Africa, but not found in areas of rain forest.
● **Size:** 13cm(5in).
● **Diet:** Foreign finch mix with spray millet, greenfood and livefood.
● **Sexing** Hens have no red markings on the head.
● **Compatibility:** Tend to be aggressive when breeding, especially towards smaller birds.

Below: **Melba Finch**
This is a cock bird. These waxbills vary in plumage across their range.

The Melba Finch, sometimes described as the Green-winged Pytilia, is probably the most familiar member of this genus of four species. It is naturally quite bold and makes an attractive aviary occupant. Individuals may differ in their plumage, because of the wide area over which this species is found. Unlike the related Aurora Finch, it is more a bird of open country. It will need careful acclimatization and access to plenty of livefood. In spite of their relatively large size, these finches are not hardy. They dislike both cold and damp weather, and in temperate climates will need to be wintered indoors in heated surroundings. Breeding details are similar to those of the Aurora Finch.

Western Bluebill
Spermophaga haematina

● **Distribution:** Tropical west Africa, extending to some central areas.
● **Size:** 15cm(6in).
● **Diet:** Small seeds such as millets and canary seed included in a foreign finch mix, plus millet sprays, seeding grasses and other greenfood. Must have livefood.
● **Sexing:** Hens are duller, with spotted and barred underparts.
● **Compatibility:** Can prove aggressive.

Above: **Western Bluebill**
Provide a densely planted flight if you hope to breed this species. It is a nervous bird by nature.

The three species of Bluebill can be recognized by the bluish shade of their beaks, but they are not well known in avicultural circles. In the wild, these finches seek the cover of vegetation and their natural nervousness can make the acclimatization phase a difficult one. Natural yoghurt offered on soaked seed may help to prevent digestive upsets in newly acquired birds. The *Lactobacillus* bacteria in the yoghurt are believed to establish a protective coat in the intestinal tract, so that harmful bacteria cannot easily become established here.

Bluebills have been bred several times in recent years. They favour a well-planted aviary, the cock birds being responsible for nest-building. Four eggs form the usual clutch. The incubation duties – lasting just over a fortnight – are shared, and fledging occurs around three weeks later. The chicks soon start feeding themselves, and can be removed from the aviary about 14 days after fledging. Offer soaked seeds and a regular supply of soft-bodied invertebrates throughout the breeding period. Adult birds may rear two clutches of chicks in succession.

Black-bellied Seedcracker

Pyrenestes ostrinus

● **Distribution:** West and Central Africa.
● **Size:** 14cm(5.5in).
● **Diet:** Foreign finch mix, millet sprays, greenfood and invertebrates.
● **Sexing:** Hens are significantly duller; in cocks the back and lower parts are generally black, but regional variations in appearance do occur.
● **Compatibility:** Can be aggressive, especially towards smaller birds.

These spectacular finches are not generally available on a regular basis, and usually command a high price. Their beak size is a variable feature, linked to the feeding habits of the birds in different localities. Seed-crackers with larger beaks may be more adept at feeding on bigger seeds with tougher casings. They require similar care to that recommended for bluebills. Be very patient when you attempt to persuade a pair of these birds to nest for the first time. It may take several years for them to settle in aviary surroundings, but a pair may nest successfully if adequate cover is provided in their aviaries. They use grass and even fern fronds to construct the breeding chamber, and lay up to five eggs, which they incubate for about 16 days.

The chicks are unlikely to fledge until they are at least three weeks old, and they may return to roost alongside the adults at night. The young seedcrackers should be independent at five weeks old.

Below: **Black-bellied Seedcracker**
The beaks of these very attractive finches vary in size, depending on the birds' natural habitat.

Peter's Twin-spot
Hypargos niveiguttatus

● **Distribution:** From eastern parts of Angola and Zaire to Mozambique and Kenya.
● **Size:** 12.5cm(5in).
● **Diet:** Foreign finch mix, greenstuff and invertebrates.
● **Sexing:** Hens are paler, with a greyish head and face.
● **Compatibility:** Some individuals can prove aggressive in a mixed collection.

A number of species of Twin-spot are occasionally available, and they make striking aviary occupants. However, they need warmth during the winter and it is only safe to keep them out of doors during the warmer months. Twin-spots are quite tame by nature, although they become secretive when breeding, preferring to nest close to or on the

Above: **Peter's Twin-spot**
Twin-spots are colourful aviary occupants, but need careful management. They are not hardy.

ground itself. Here they may line a suitable depression with a little nesting material before laying, disguising the location as much as possible. Avoid interfering with breeding birds, since they may desert their nest. Clutch size can vary from three to six eggs, which should hatch within a fortnight. Fledging occurs three weeks later, but you must provide an adequate supply of livefood during this time.

Other Twin-spots may be available from time to time; these include the Green-backed (*Mandingoa nitidula*), of which Schlegel's (*M.n. schlegeli*) is the best-known race, and Dybowski's (*Euschistospiza Dybowskii*). All require similar care.

Senegal Firefinch
Lagonosticta senegala

● **Distribution:** Found over much of Africa, south of the Sahara.
● **Size:** 11.5cm(4.5in).
● **Diet:** Foreign finch mix, including millet sprays, plus invertebrates and greenstuff.
● **Sexing:** Cocks have reddish brown backs, whereas hens are duller overall.
● **Compatibility:** Not usually aggressive in a mixed collection.

There are eight species of firefinches, so-named because of the reddish tones in their plumage. They can be difficult birds to acclimatize, and – for their first year at least – need to be kept warm over the winter. Even then you should still provide heat and light unless the climate is very mild.

Once established, however, pairs of firefinches nest readily and can prove prolific in suitable aviary surroundings. A typical clutch will consist of four eggs, which should hatch after an incubation period of 12 days. Fledging will take a further three weeks. It may be possible to

Above: **Senegal Firefinch**
The reddish plumage coloration, particularly of male birds, has given rise to their common name.

recognize young cocks even at this stage, as they can show a reddish tinge to their plumage.

They do not seem to rank among the most long-lived of the waxbills; this may be a reflection of their high reproductive rate.

Red-cheeked Cordon Bleu
Uraeginthus bengalus

● **Distribution:** Across much of southern Africa.
● **Size:** 12.5cm(5in).
● **Diet:** Foreign finch mix, with greenfood and invertebrates.
● **Sexing:** Hens tend to be paler, with less prominent blue plumage.
● **Compatibility:** May become aggressive when nesting.

The Red-cheeked is the most distinctive of the three species of Cordon Bleu, but only cocks possess the characteristic red cheek patches. The other species are the Blue-capped Cordon Bleu (*U. cyanocephalus*) and the Blue-breasted (*U. angolensis*), which require similar care.

When you first acquire Cordon Bleus they will need careful management and a diet that includes suitable invertebrates. Transfer them to an outside aviary when the weather is mild, and bring them into heated accommodation for the following winter.

Cordon Bleus will often use a closed wicker nesting basket in the aviary. Livefood is vital for the successful rearing of chicks, since parents will often eject chicks from the nest if there is a shortage. If you find a young chick outside the nest, do not automatically assume that it is dead; you may be able to revive it by warming it in your hands for a few minutes. Transfer the chick back to the nest and, as long as you modify the birds' diet to include suitable livefood, all the chicks may be reared successfully.

Above: **Blue-breasted Waxbills**
Once acclimatized, Cordon Bleu Waxbills may prove long lived, but they need heat and light in winter.

Below: **Red-cheeked Cordon Bleu**
These distinctive finches make a colourful addition to the aviary.

Violet-eared Waxbill
Uraeginthus granatina

● **Distribution:** Extending from Angola and Mozambique to Natal and into Cape Province.
● **Size:** 12.5cm(5in).
● **Diet:** Foreign finch mix, including millet sprays, livefood and greenfood.
● **Sexing:** Hens are significantly paler than cocks.
● **Compatibility:** Liable to be aggressive, especially when breeding.

This species and the closely related Purple Grenadier (*U. ianthinogaster*) are highly insectivorous throughout the year, although they will occasionally take other sources of protein, such as a little grated cheese on top of softfood.

In spite of their attractive coloration, these two species of waxbill cannot be recommended

Above: **Violet-eared Waxbill**
A striking waxbill that needs regular livefood if it is to stay in top condition and breed.

for the novice owner. They can be difficult to establish, and their aggressive natures mean that they are best housed in individual pairs on their own. Furthermore, both Violet-eared and Purple Grenadier Waxbills must be kept in heated winter quarters.

When breeding, a pair usually choose a site low down in bushes. They use grass to build a nest, and line the inside with feathers. A clutch may consist of up to five eggs, which are incubated by both adults. Hatching should occur after about 13 days, at which stage these waxbills become almost entirely insectivorous. Fledging takes place three weeks later, and the young waxbills will be feeding themselves within a further 14 days.

Lavender Finch
Estrilda caerulescens

● **Distribution:** From Senegal to southwest Chad and northern Cameroon.
● **Size:** 10cm(4in).
● **Diet:** Foreign finch mix, with invertebrates and greenfood.
● **Sexing:** Hens may be smaller than cocks and somewhat paler in coloration.
● **Compatibility:** Can be kept as part of a mixed collection.

The plumage of imported Lavender Finches is often poor, since these birds tend to pluck themselves when kept together in cages. In this condition they require considerable care, and you should release them into an outside aviary only when their plumage has regrown. A varied diet with a nutritional supplement will help the birds to settle down.

Lavender Finches prove lively aviary occupants, and nest quite readily. They often use fairly long pieces of grass and other plant stems, such as those of Shepherd's Purse (*Capsella bursa-pastoris*), to build the external fabric of their nest and line the interior with feathers and softer items. Clutch size can vary from four to six eggs and the incubation period is about 12 days, with both adults sitting during this time. The young waxbills may leave the nest for the first time when only 16 days old but the fledging period may last longer. This need not be a cause for concern; the chicks will leave the nest in due course, and should not be disturbed. Breeding details are similar for other *Estrilda* species.

Below: **Lavender Finch**
In confined surroundings these finches may pluck themselves; house at first in an indoor flight.

Black-cheeked Waxbill

Estrilda erythronotos

● **Distribution:** East Africa, in Tanzania, Uganda and Kenya, and further south in South Africa, Angola, Zimbabwe and Zambia.
● **Size:** 11.5cm(4.5in).
● **Diet:** Foreign finch mix, with greenstuff and invertebrates.
● **Sexing:** Hens have paler markings on the flanks and appear less reddish, although regional variations in the form of subspecies are recognized.
● **Compatibility:** Normally safe to keep with related species.

There are several species of waxbill with black head markings, and it can be difficult to distinguish between them. The Pink-bellied form (*E. charmosyna*) occurs further north, in northeastern Africa and, as its name suggests, has more pinkish underparts.

It appears that in the wild these species may feed in part on pollen grains collected from flowers. It may be worthwhile including this item in the diet, particularly for newly acquired birds, as they can be difficult to establish. Pollen in granular form is available from many health food stores, and you can either sprinkle it over soaked seed or dissolve it in a nectar solution. Proprietary brands of

nectar marketed for softbills can also be useful for finches; make up a fresh solution each day. Nectar is easily absorbed into the body and can be a valuable tonic. Livefood is also important for these naturally insectivorous waxbills.

Orange-cheeked Waxbill

Estrilda melpoda

● **Distribution:** West Africa.
● **Size:** 10cm(4in).
● **Diet:** Foreign finch mix, livefood and greenfood.
● **Sexing:** In some cases hens are paler and have a small area of orange coloration on the sides of the head.
● **Compatibility:** May be disruptive when breeding.

These attractive waxbills are often available but, unfortunately, can prove rather nervous unless their flight is well planted. They normally inhabit areas of grassland, where it is easy for them to conceal themselves. Orange-cheeked Waxbills are not entirely hardy, even once established, and are best overwintered indoors. If a pair choose to nest in an aviary, avoid disturbing them, otherwise they may desert their nest.

Below: **Black-cheeked Waxbill**
This species may appreciate pollen granules sprinkled over softfood.

Above: **Orange-cheeked Waxbill**
Often available and easy to cater for, but usually proves nervous.

In common with other related species, their nest is a relatively bulky structure. An interesting feature is the so-called 'cock's nest' above, which is relatively conspicuous, yet never occupied. This serves to confuse potential predators, since the real entrance to the breeding chamber beneath is hidden on the side of the nest and often disguised with a feather.

St. Helena Waxbill
Estrilda astrild

● **Distribution:** Occurs over much of southern Africa.
● **Size:** 11.5cm(4.5in).
● **Diet:** Foreign finch mix, with greenstuff and livefood.
● **Sexing:** The abdomen of the cock is a deeper pink.
● **Compatibility:** Tends to be less social than related species.

This waxbill, sometimes known simply as the Common Waxbill, is one of the easiest species to keep and breed successfully, and thus makes a good introduction to this group of birds. However, it still needs careful acclimatization and must be kept warm during the cold winter months.

St. Helena Waxbills are less dependent on livefood for rearing purposes than other waxbills, and may even be conditioned to take softfoods of various types when they have chicks. Young birds can be recognized by their blackish beaks. They will moult into adult plumage for the first time when they are about two months old.

Below: **St. Helena Waxbill**
This adaptable species will breed in captivity; it often chooses a nesting site close to the ground.

Red-eared Waxbill
Estrilda troglodytes

● **Distribution:** Found in a broad band across Africa, in semi-arid areas from Senegal and the Gambia to Uganda, Sudan and Ethiopia.
● **Size:** 10cm(4in).
● **Diet:** Foreign finch mix, plus livefood and greenfood.
● **Sexing:** Females tend to be paler, especially on the belly, but this is not an entirely reliable guide.
● **Compatibility:** Quite tolerant in a mixed collection.

Red-eared Waxbills are among the most freely available species, and invariably look attractive, remaining sleek even in cage surroundings. However, these birds are very active and fare better in an aviary. During the warmer months of the year, a group will generally breed successfully in an outside aviary. Sexing is difficult, but it is usually possible to recognize cock birds in breeding condition by their display. They hold some nesting material, such as blades of grass, in their beaks while bobbing up and down in front of a hen. As in the case of the Red-eared Cordon Bleu, a dilute mutation of this species has been recorded, where the beak is orange and the pink parts of the body are similarly diluted.

Below: **Red-eared Waxbill**
These diminutive birds always look in good condition. They thrive on a good seed mixture plus livefood.

Green Avadavat
Amandava formosa

● **Distribution:** India.
● **Size:** 10cm(4in).
● **Diet:** Foreign finch mixture, with greenfood and livefood.
● **Sexing:** Hens may be duller in coloration than cocks.
● **Compatibility:** Can be aggressive, especially towards birds of similar coloration. This applies also to the related Red Avadavat (*A. amandava*).

The avadavats are known by a variety of common names, such as the Green Munia in the case of this species, or the Tiger Finch, or Red Munia, which are alternative names for the Red Avadavat. Both originate from Asia and are similar in their habits, which closely resemble those of African waxbills.

Like its red counterpart, the Green Avadavat can prove free breeding once established in its quarters. Again, you will need to provide an adequate supply of invertebrates if chicks are to be reared successfully. Some pairs may even nest in cages, but in

Above: **Red Avadavat**
This colourful Asiatic species is ideal for the novice finchkeeper.

these surroundings it is not unusual for Red Avadavats to develop blackish plumage. A varied diet and an outdoor aviary that offers more spacious accommodation may help to resolve this abnormality at the next moult.

Gold-breasted Waxbill
Amandava subflava

● **Distribution:** Most of Africa, south of the Sahara Desert.
● **Size:** 9cm(3.5in).
● **Diet:** Foreign finch mix. Offer livefood and greenfood as well.
● **Sexing:** Hens are duller and lack the red eye stripe associated with cock birds.
● **Compatibility:** Sociable.

The Gold-breasted Waxbill from Africa is the third member of the *Amandava* genus and one of the smallest waxbills. To ensure that its accommodation is suitably secure, use mesh measuring 1.25cm(0.5in) square for cages and aviaries. Pairs will nest in a typical waxbill fashion and may prove quite prolific, providing you supply the usual rearing foods, including livefood and soaked seeds. In aviary surroundings where the birds cannot build their own nests, supply branches of gorse or nesting baskets. Gold-breasted Waxbills are reasonably hardy once acclimatized, but provide moderate heat and artificial lighting if you keep them in a birdroom during the winter months.

Below: **Gold-breasted Waxbill**
These small waxbills are very attractive and often nest readily.

Quail-finch
Ortygosiza atricollis

● **Distribution:** There are two
distinct populations: one occurs in
West Africa, while the other is
found in eastern and southern parts
of Africa.
● **Size:** 10cm(4in).
● **Diet:** Foreign finch mix, plus
invertebrates and greenfood.
● **Sexing** Females tend to be both
duller and paler than cocks.
● **Compatibility:** Cocks can be
aggressive towards each other and
towards other ground-dwelling
birds, such as the Chinese Painted
Quail (*Excalfactoria chinensis*).

These unusual waxbills spend
much of their time on the floor of
their quarters, rarely flying unless
flushed from the grass or
frightened, in which case they tend
to take off vertically. Study of their
behavioural patterns has
suggested that quail-finches are
most closely related to the
Amandava waxbills. In aviary
surroundings, they will add
considerable interest to a planted
flight, although you will have to
bring them indoors over the winter.
  Provided that adequate cover is
available, a pair will often attempt
to nest. A typical clutch consists of
five eggs, which should start to
hatch after about two weeks.
Fledging usually takes place by the
time the chicks are three weeks old.
Suitable invertebrates form a

Above: **Quail-finch**
*A semi-terrestrial species that often
nests close to the ground.*

significant part of the diet of these
finches when they are rearing
chicks. Whiteworm is a popular
livefood, but the birds also catch
aquatic midges and their larvae.
You can culture these by leaving a
bowl of water out of doors, and
here the midges will lay their eggs.
Once the larvae have hatched,
drain the water through a sieve and
offer the larvae to the finches in a
very shallow pot of water.

Diamond Firetail
Emblema guttata

● **Distribution:** Eastern Australia.
● **Size:** 11.5cm(4.5in).
● **Diet:** A mixture of the small
cereal seeds, including spray millet,
plus greenfood and livefood.
● **Sexing:** Hens may be smaller
and duller in coloration, especially
around the head.
● **Compatibility:** Some individuals
are more aggressive than others.

The unpredictable temperament of
the Diamond Firetail, or Diamond
Sparrow as it is sometimes known,
means that pairs may have to be
kept on their own. Unfortunately, in
the confines of a cage, they prove
inactive and prone to obesity.
  Compatibility is an important
factor in successful breeding, since

not all true pairs will nest readily. If you encounter problems, swap the partners round or, better still, house a group together and remove those birds which have clearly paired up, watching carefully for any signs of aggression.

The birds choose a site quite close to the ground and build a large nest in a nestbox, or possibly in a suitable shrub in an aviary. Between four and six eggs form the usual clutch, and the shared incubation period lasts 13 days. Offer softfood and soaked seed throughout the rearing phase. Although livefood is not essential for rearing purposes, it will certainly improve the likelihood of success. The young birds leave the nest at about three weeks old.

Below: **Diamond Firetail**
Take care that these birds do not become obese in cages.

Star Finch
Poephila ruficauda

● **Distribution:** Northwestern Australia, extending eastwards to parts of Queensland.
● **Size:** 10cm(4in).
● **Diet:** A mixture of the smaller cereal seeds, including spray millet, plus greenfood and possibly some livefood.
● **Sexing:** Hens are duller overall; the area of red on the face is paler and smaller than in cocks.
● **Compatibility:** Reasonably tolerant.

Pairs of these Australian finches usually nest quite readily, in both cage and aviary surroundings. They may lay up to six eggs in one clutch, and the adult birds share the incubation, which lasts 13 days. The parents may not start to sit in earnest until the hen has laid three eggs. This behaviour is quite normal, and simply ensures that the chicks will be of similar age when they hatch. Star Finches will accept livefood if it is offered, but can rear their offspring without it.

Two mutant forms have been recorded, of which the Yellow-headed is the best known. There are reports of an Albino mutation.

Below: **Star Finch**
This is an ideal aviary occupant and a good introduction to the care of Australian grassfinches.

Zebra Finch
Poephila guttata

● **Distribution:** Occurs over much of Australia, apart from the Cape York Peninsula and southern coastal districts. Also absent from Tasmania, but found on the Flores Islands, to the northwest of Australia.
● **Size:** 10cm(4in).
● **Diet:** Millets and canary seed, plus greenfood.
● **Sexing:** Hens lack the zebra-like patterning on the cock's throat and the chestnut flank markings.
● **Compatibility:** Can be kept in groups or as part of a mixed collection.

The Zebra Finch is one of the most popular species of finch in birdkeeping circles throughout the world, and various colour mutations are well established. Pure white Zebra Finches were known by the early 1920s and, even though the typical markings which distinguish the cock bird are missing, they can be recognized by their darker red beaks. The Albino, which is also pure white, has red

Above: **Zebra Finch**
This is a normal cock bird, showing the characteristic area of black and white markings on the throat.

eyes. It remains a scarce mutation. The other white variant is the Chestnut-flanked White (CFW), where the typical markings of the cock bird are retained, while the remainder of the body is white.

Below: **White Zebra Finch**
In this case, the difference in beak coloration is a guide to distinguishing the sexes. Hens have paler red beaks than cock birds.

In the Pied mutation, first bred in 1935 in Denmark, the patterning is irregular, with some birds showing more white than dark areas in their plumage. Fawn Pieds have also been developed, using the Fawn mutation. This by itself creates a warm brown shade, replacing the Zebra Finch's normal greyish plumage. Combining the diluting effect of the Silver mutation with the Fawn has given rise to the Cream Zebra Finch. Both recessive and dominant forms of the Silver and Cream mutations exist; birds of the recessive type tend to be slightly darker in their overall coloration.

The Crested mutation occurs independently of colour, as does a mutation affecting the beak, turning it yellow rather than red. Birds of this latter type are relatively scarce at present, as are other mutations that are still being developed, but they may well become more widely available in the future.

Zebra finches nest readily, in both cage and aviary surroundings, adopting either a domed wicker basket or a nestbox. Once they have laid, remove any unused nesting material, since the birds may continue building the nest and bury their eggs in the process. For the same reason it is a good idea to chop greenfood into small pieces. Up to six eggs form the usual clutch, and both parents share the

Above: **Crested Zebra Finch**
The Crested mutation can be combined with any colour, but such birds must not be paired together because of the lethal factor.

incubation of about 12 days. No livefood is required once the chicks hatch, but you should certainly encourage the adult birds to take softfood beforehand, so that this forms the basis of the rearing diet. Since they are used to feeding on it they will accept it readily once they have chicks. Fledging occurs when the chicks are about 18 days old and they will be feeding independently within a fortnight.

Below: **Chestnut-flanked White**
Here, the typical markings of the cock bird are retained, together with otherwise white plumage. An attractive colour combination.

Bicheno Finch
Poephila bichenovii

● **Distribution:** Northern and eastern parts of Australia.
● **Size:** 11.5cm(4.5in).
● **Diet:** A mixture of millets and canary seed, with greenfood and some invertebrates.
● **Sexing:** No clear visual distinction between the sexes.
● **Compatibility:** Not usually aggressive.

This attractive species is sometimes described as the Owl Finch, because of the dark head markings. It does not differ significantly from related grassfinches in its requirements, but compatibility may be a problem with some breeding pairs. You can rear the birds successfully on a colony system, which will allow them to select their own partners. Some pairs choose to line their nests with feathers, but studies in the wild have shown that this seems to be a geographical characteristic. Bicheno Finches are intolerant of cold wet weather and will need to be kept indoors over the winter in most areas.

Below: **Bicheno Finch**
Also known as the Owl finch because of the head patterning.

Long-tailed Grassfinch
Poephila acuticauda

● **Distribution:** Northern Australia.
● **Size:** 11.5cm(4.5in).
● **Diet:** A mixture of millets and canary seed, with greenfood and livefood.
● **Sexing:** In some cases it is possible to distinguish a hen bird by the smaller area of black plumage on the breast.
● **Compatibility:** Not usually aggressive.

These grassfinches are quite readily available, and pairs normally nest freely. Indeed, it may be necessary to restrict them to just three broods during the course of a year. They should develop a strong pair bond, but if they prove reluctant to nest, then swapping partners may have the desired effect. Two distinctive subspecies are recognized: the nominate race, known as the Yellow-billed, occurs in the western part of the range, while the red-beaked form, *P.a. hecki*, sometimes called Heck's Grassfinch, is found in eastern areas. Avoid pairing these distinctive forms together. A fawn mutation of Heck's Grassfinch has recently been recorded. Closely related to these grassfinches is Parson's Finch (*P. cincta*); both

Above: **Long-tailed grassfinch**
*Beak colour is a guide to different
races; the red beak of this bird
identifies it as Heck's Grassfinch.*

fawn and white mutations of
P. cincta have been recorded. The
Masked Grassfinch (*P. personata*)
has similar habits.

Gouldian Finch
Chloebia gouldiae

● **Distribution:** Northern parts of
Australia.
● **Size:** 12.5cm(5in).
● **Diet:** A mixture of the smaller
cereal seeds with greenfood.
● **Sexing:** Hens tend to be lighter
in overall coloration. When cock
birds are in breeding condition,
their beaks turn reddish at the tip,
whereas those of hens become
darker overall.
● **Compatibility:** Will live together
well in groups.

The Gouldian Finch – the most
colourful of the Australian finches –
is a very popular avicultural subject.
Its head coloration is variable, even
in the wild. Both black and red-
headed forms are common, but the
so-called yellow-headed form –
more accurately described as the
orange-headed – is normally
scarce. It is possible to find birds of
all these different colours in the
same flock, with black-headed
variants being most numerous.
Study of the genetics of these
forms, however, has revealed that

the Red-headed variant is actually
dominant over the Black-headed
form of Gouldian Finch.
   Various other colour forms have
been developed in captivity. There
is a white-breasted mutation,
where the normal purple breast
coloration is replaced by white
plumage, and a paler lilac-breasted
form. These can be combined with
any head coloration.
· In Europe, Gouldian Finches are
usually bred in cages and they will
use either a domed nesting basket
or an open-fronted nestbox. A hen
can lay up to six eggs in a clutch,
and these should start to hatch
after a period of 16 days.
   Soaked seed is important during
the rearing phase, along with
greenfood and softfoods. When
they leave the nest, young Gouldian
Finches are significantly duller than
adults. Slow weaning may help to
minimize the risk of 'going light', to
which these birds are susceptible
(see page 55). As with other related
species, these finches are not
hardy, and must be kept in heated
surroundings during the winter.

Below: **Yellow-headed Gouldian**
*This is a dilute variant of the Red-
headed, which is genetically
dominant over the Black-headed
form. A rare mutation in the wild,
but a striking aviary subject.*

Pin-tailed Nonpareil
Erythrura prasina

● **Distribution:** Thailand and Malaya to Sumatra, Java and Borneo.
● **Size:** 14cm(5.5in).
● **Diet:** Foreign finch mix, with other seeds, such as paddy rice, groats and hemp added in moderation.
● **Sexing:** Hens lack the red on the belly and have a reduced area of blue on their faces. A yellow-bellied mutation has occurred in the wild.
● **Compatibility:** Social by nature.

In the wild, these parrot-finches congregate in large flocks, plundering rice crops throughout their native range. If you have difficulty establishing these birds in captivity, it is a good idea, to add paddy rice to their diet.

Above: **Pin-tailed Nonpareil**
These attractive parrot-finches are generally available, but may be difficult to acclimatize.

The best way of encouraging breeding activity is to keep these finches in a group in an indoor flight, and offer them a selection of nesting sites. Breeding results in captivity are not common, but it appears that Pin-tailed Nonpareils favour a nestbox and may use coconut fibres and moss to construct a nesting chamber within. Between two and five eggs form the usual clutch and these hatch after an incubation period of a fortnight. The adults tend to cease brooding their young before the chicks are fully feathered; ideally, keep pairs in heated surroundings and maintain the temperature at around 25°C(77°F).

Blue-faced Parrot-finch
Erythrura trichroa

● **Distribution:** Northeastern Australia, New Guinea and neighbouring islands, including the Celebes and Moluccas east to the New Hebrides and Loyalty Islands.
● **Size:** 11.5cm(4.5in).
● **Diet:** A mixture of the smaller cereal seeds, especially canary seed, plus soaked seeds, greenfood and invertebrates.
● **Sexing:** Hens have a smaller and duller area of blue on their faces than cocks.
● **Compatibility:** Keep pairs of the same species apart, but you can house them with other finches of similar size.

At present this species is the best-known example of parrot-finch in avicultural collections. In view of its nervous nature, you should keep it only in aviary surroundings. In a planted flight, pairs usually settle down well and are likely to breed. They often prefer to use a nestbox rather than a wicker basket, and favour dried grass as nesting material. After a fairly violent courtship, the hen will lay about five eggs, but clutches of up to eight eggs have been reported. The incubation period will last for about 14 days, and the chicks will fledge at around three weeks old. Once they have fledged, they will not return to the nest. Within 10 days, the young parrot-finches will be independent and you should remove them from their parents at this stage before they are persecuted by the adult cock.

Blue-headed Parrot-finches can be prolific; records show that a single pair have successfully reared up to 39 chicks in under 18 months. In order not to tax the hen's stamina unduly, you may need to prevent pairs nesting excessively by moving them to indoor accommodation in late autumn.

Below: **Blue-faced Parrot-finch**
A rather nervous bird that does best when kept in a planted aviary. Pairs may prove prolific breeders.

White-headed Nun
Lonchura maja

● **Distribution:** Malaysia and surrounding islands.
● **Size:** 11.5cm(4.5in).
● **Diet:** A mixture of the smaller cereal seeds, including paddy rice, with greenfood.
● **Sexing:** No visual means of distinction possible.
● **Compatibility:** Agree well in groups, and with related birds of similar size.

These attractive finches are known by a variety of common names, including Pale-headed Munia and White-headed Mannikin. They are relatively easy birds to cater for since, like related species, they are capable of rearing their chicks with little or no livefood, although soaked seed is a valuable addition to the diet at this time. Breeding success is far more likely in a planted flight, where a pair can construct their own nest in a suitable bush. The birds use dried grass to build the nest and leave a hole on the side of the structure for access. They may lay up to seven eggs inside and the parents share the incubation duties, which last about 13 days. The young fledge at about three weeks old.

Below: **White-headed Nun**
A hardy and long-lived species once established in a planted aviary.

Tri-coloured Nun
Lonchura malacca

● **Distribution:** From India across Southeast Asia to the Philippines and other offshore islands, including the Celebes.
● **Size:** 11.5cm(4.5in).
● **Diet:** A mixture of the smaller cereal seeds, with paddy rice and greenfood.
● **Sexing:** No reliable visual distinctions possible.
● **Compatibility:** Agree well in groups and with related birds of similar size.

This species does not differ significantly from the White-headed Nun in its requirements. Keep a check on the claws, which often become overgrown. These birds often show a preference for nesting in bamboo, so it is worth including this plant in the aviary to increase the likelihood of breeding success.

Tri-coloured Nuns may differ somewhat in appearance; 10 subspecies are recognized throughout their wide range. Indeed, there is some dispute over the status of some of these races and they are sometimes grouped with the Black-headed Nun (*L. atricapilla*) under the common name of Chestnut Nun or Munia.

Above: **Tri-coloured Nun**
These mannikins and related species thrive well in a group.

Below: **Spice Finch**
These popular mannikins are often available, and prove reasonably hardy once settled in the aviary.

Spice Finch
Lonchura punctulata

● **Distribution:** From India extending to much of Southeast Asia into China and Malaysia.
● **Size:** 10cm(4in).
● **Diet:** A mixture of the smaller cereal seeds, with paddy rice, greenfood and livefood.
● **Sexing:** No reliable visual distinctions possible.
● **Compatibility:** Agree well in groups, and with related birds of similar size.

Another Asiatic munia, the Spice Bird – or Nutmeg Finch, as it is also known – tends to be more insectivorous when breeding than the previous species. Pairs will nest readily in a domed nesting basket that they line with dried grass, but they are not averse to building a complete nest from scratch if there is suitable vegetation in the aviary. Breeding details are similar to those of the White-headed Nun; once again, soaked seed is a valuable rearing food. These finches are relatively hardy once acclimatized.

93

African Silverbill
Lonchura malabarica cantans

● **Distribution:** Northern Africa, ranging from Senegal eastwards to Sudan.
● **Size:** 10cm(4in).
● **Diet:** Foreign finch mix plus greenfood.
● **Sexing:** No reliable visual distinction possible, although hens may be slightly smaller, with reddish tails.
● **Compatibility:** Social by nature. Can be kept with waxbills.

Two forms of this silverbill are recognized; the Indian Silverbill (*L.m. malabarica*) has a white rump, whereas in the African race this part of the body is black. Both forms require similar care and, although not especially colourful, they are lively and attractive aviary occupants. Pairs will nest readily and, in common with other munias, cock silverbills will both sing and display to their mates at breeding time – a clear way of recognizing the males. Silverbills have occasionally been used to foster the eggs and young of other species, but such transfers have not always proved successful. Silverbills do not require livefood when breeding, but encourage them to take a softfood, if possible, along with soaked seed.

Bronze-winged Mannikin
Lonchura cucullata

● **Distribution:** Found over much of Africa, apart from southwestern regions.
● **Size:** 10cm(4in).
● **Diet:** A mixture of the smaller cereal seeds.
● **Sexing:** No reliable visual distinctions possible.
● **Compatibility:** Tend to be more aggressive than their Asiatic relatives.

These are the most commonly available of the African mannikins. Although they are not generally pugnacious, they do tend to dominate other birds sharing their accommodation, especially during the breeding period. Bronze-winged Mannikins are, therefore, best kept in a group on their own. They are undemanding in terms of nesting accommodation, happily adopting a basket or box for the purpose, and breeding details do not differ significantly from those of related species. They may accept livefood during the rearing period.

Left: **African Silverbill**
Pairs of silverbills will often attempt to nest. The male bird sings and displays to his mate.

Above: **Bronze-winged Mannikin**
The African mannikins are less commonly available than the Asian species and can be more aggressive.

Other African mannikins, such as the large Magpie Mannikin (*L. fringilloides*) need similar care, but these birds may become quite belligerent towards other species, particularly when nesting.

Pearl-headed Silverbill
Lonchura caniceps

● **Distribution:** Eastern Africa, from southern Ethiopia to Kenya and Tanzania.
● **Size:** 11.5cm(4.5in).
● **Diet:** Foreign finch mix, plus greenfood and some livefood.
● **Sexing:** No reliable visual distinctions possible.
● **Compatibility:** Social by nature.

These silverbills, sometimes known as Grey-headed Silverbills, are not as common as the previous species, but are equally easy to look after. It is easy to distinguish young birds, since they lack the white facial spots evident in adults. Like other silverbills, this species will use the old nests of waxbills if a suitable opportunity presents itself. Breeding details do not differ significantly from those of the White-headed Nun (see page 92). These birds will accept livefood, especially when there are chicks in the nest.

Below: **Pearl-headed Silverbill**
These handsome birds show a readiness to breed once settled in.

Bengalese Finch
Lonchura domestica

● **Distribution:** Does not occur in the wild.
● **Size:** 10cm(4in).
● **Diet:** Smaller cereal seeds, including millet sprays and greenstuff.
● **Sexing:** No reliable visual distinction possible.
● **Compatibility:** Social by nature.

It seems likely that Bengalese, or Society, Finches are a domesticated form of the White-backed Munia (*L. striata*), which originated in China several centuries ago. Bengalese Finches were first seen in Europe, during 1860, when the London Zoo received a pair of white Bengalese. These birds provide a good introduction for the inexperienced finchkeeper and also offer considerable scope for the keen specialist and exhibitor.

Several mutations are recognized. Bearing in mind the coloration of its probable ancestor, it seems likely that the natural form of the Bengalese is the Self Chocolate. The term 'self' refers to an unbroken pattern of coloration, since such birds have no white feathers among their normal plumage. Self Fawn Bengalese are lighter in coloration, and recently the Self Chestnut form has become much more common. At first, this was simply believed to be a dilute version of the Self Chocolate, but it is now accepted as a separate mutation. The ideal coloration of the Self Chestnut should be midway between the Self Chocolate and the Self Fawn. All three colours can also be obtained in a pied form, displaying variable degrees of white plumage. The dilute factor can also affect all the coloured forms, while a crested variant can be introduced, independently of colour. The white form of the Bengalese is rare; such birds tend to be smaller than normal and, if red-eyed, are described as Albinos.

At first, keep Bengalese Finches in groups until you can recognize pairs. Like other munias, cocks will sing and display to intended mates. The birds will breed readily in both cage and aviary surroundings and generally prove diligent parents. In

Below: **Self Fawn Bengalese**
Bengalese are known as Society Finches in North America. They are sociable and easy to cater for.

a few cases, a hen may lay up to nine eggs in a clutch. Provide eggfood and similar items for rearing purposes.

Bengalese make good exhibition subjects. Specific standards are established for various mutations; in the case of pieds, for example, birds with an even distribution of colour and white areas are favoured on the show bench.

Above: **Fawn and White Bengalese**
Bengalese are popular exhibition subjects and are also highly valued as foster parents for the eggs and chicks of other birds.

Below: **Self Chocolate Bengalese**
Self birds, irrespective of the variety, should show no white feathers in their plumage. This is the darkest form available.

Java Sparrow
Lonchura oryzivora

● **Distribution:** Believed to have originated on the islands of Bali and Java, but has since spread over a much wider area, including Malaysia, the Moluccas, the Philippines and other Asian localities.
● **Size:** 14cm(5.5in).
● **Diet:** Small cereal seeds, plus paddy rice, greenfood and livefood.
● **Sexing:** No clear-cut plumage distinctions, but cocks may develop an enlarged lower mandible when in breeding condition.
● **Compatibility:** Agree well in groups, or with other munias.

In the wild, these munias inhabit rice-growing areas, where they can cause considerable damage. In the United States they are also known as Rice Birds. The birds are more likely to breed if a group is housed in a flight, although often under these circumstances, only a dominant pair will actually breed. Java Sparrows lay their eggs in budgerigar nestboxes; a typical clutch consists of between four and six eggs, which should hatch after about a fortnight. The young chicks will leave the nest by the age of one month and will be independent within a further three weeks. They will moult into adult plumage at around three months old.

Above: **Fawn Java Sparrow**
This Australian mutation retains its sleek plumage throughout life. Mutations may breed more readily.

Java Sparrows always look immaculate, even when moulting, and this is also a feature of the various mutations that are now established. The white form is relatively common, but pied markings are often evident, especially in recently fledged youngsters. A more recent introduction is the fawn mutation, which emerged initially in Australia during the late 1950s. It has since become quite common in Europe and elsewhere.

Left: **Normal Java Sparrow**
These birds are called Rice Birds in North America. They are quite hardy and agree well in groups.

Cut-throat
Amadina fasciata

● **Distribution:** Northern and eastern parts of Africa, extending southwards to Mozambique.
● **Size:** 12.5cm(5in).
● **Diet:** Smaller cereal seeds, including millet sprays, plus greenfood and livefood.
● **Sexing:** Hens lack the bright red throat markings of the cocks.
● **Compatibility:** May be aggressive when breeding. Safe companions generally for munias, but do not keep with waxbills.

The Cut-throat is easy to sex, and pairs will nest quite readily. However, hens are prone to egg-binding (see *Breeding and rearing*, page 52), and must have access to adequate sources of calcium. Prevent them from breeding while

Below: **Cut-throat**
Note the characteristic red throat markings of the cock bird.

the weather remains cold, and after they have reared two clutches of chicks in a season. Do not encourage young birds to breed until they themselves are fully mature, at about one year.

Like other birds, notably sparrows, Cut-throats will engage in 'dust bathing'. They seek out an area of dry soil and scratch the earth in among their plumage. The reason for such behaviour is unclear; it may help to remove parasites or excessive natural oil from the plumage. In aviary surroundings, offer these birds a tray of dry soil for this purpose. A seed tray with a solid base, placed on the floor of the aviary, makes an ideal container.

The related Red-headed Finch (*A. erythrocephala*) is bred less often, but is sometimes available; it needs the same care as the Cut-throat. Although both species are relatively hardy once acclimatized, neither like prolonged spells of cold wet weather.

Family: VIDUINAE – Parasitic whydahs and weavers
A family in which the sexes can be easily distinguished. Hens lay their eggs in the nests of other birds. Some have very specific parasitic habits.

Queen Whydah
Vidua regia

● **Distribution:** Southern Angola and Zimbabwe, extending to Cape Province.
● **Size:** Cocks in colour can measure 33cm(13in) overall, averaging 11.5cm(4.5in) during the rest of the year.
● **Diet:** Typical foreign finch mix, plus greenfood and some livefood.
● **Sexing:** Cocks are instantly recognizable by their nuptial plumage. Out of colour, their plumage tends to be darker than that of hens.
● **Compatibility:** Keep whydahs alongside waxbills for breeding purposes.

Always house these striking birds in flights, where their long tails will not be damaged and where you can fully appreciate their lively natures. Breeding is difficult, since hens are parasitic by nature, laying their eggs in the nests of specific waxbills. The Violet-eared Waxbill is the usual host species for these particular whydahs and both whydah and waxbill must be in breeding condition in the same aviary. The waxbills will rear the whydah chicks alongside their own. The markings inside the mouths of the young whydahs match those of the host species, so that the foster parents cannot distinguish the whydahs from their own chicks.

Below: **Queen Whydah**
A pair of these birds, with the cock in breeding plumage, as shown by his magnificent long tail plumes. These are not difficult to keep.

Pin-tailed Whydah
Vidua macroura

● **Distribution:** Over much of Africa, southwards from Senegal.
● **Size:** Cocks in colour can measure 38cm(15in) overall, averaging 11.5cm(4.5in) for the rest of the year.
● **Diet:** Typical foreign finch mix, plus greenfood and some livefood.
● **Sexing:** Cocks are instantly reconizable by their nuptial plumage. Out of colour, their plumage tends to be darker than that of hens.
● **Compatibility:** Keep whydahs alongside waxbills for breeding purposes, including the St. Helena, Red-eared and Orange-cheeked.

Above: **Pin-tailed Whydah**
Another cock bird in breeding finery. A parasitic species.

Normally, the *Vidua* species lay their eggs in the nests of specific waxbill hosts, but the Pin-tailed Whydah is an exception. Records show that it has layed in the nests of as many as 19 species. For breeding purposes, house several hens and one cock together alongside waxbills. Co-ordinating the breeding activities of waxbills and whydahs can be difficult, but this species is undoubtedly one of the easiest to breed under aviary conditions. Whydahs can prove long-lived birds, and may survive well into their teens.

101

Senegal Combassou
Vidua chalybeata

● **Distribution:** Over much of Africa, south of the Sahara to Botswana.
● **Size:** 10cm(4in).
● **Diet:** Foreign finch mix, with greenfood and some livefood.
● **Sexing:** Cocks in colour are bluish black. Out of colour, they resemble hens, but can be distinguished by their darker head markings.
● **Compatibility:** Can be housed alongside waxbills.

Combassous are sometimes advertised as indigo birds, which is

Above: **Senegal Combassou**
Although not as striking as other whydahs, combassous are delightful aviary occupants. House them with firefinches (Lagonosticta sp.) *to boost breeding chances.*

a reference to the distinctive coloration of the cock in breeding condition, but generally they are not as striking as the other *Vidua* species. These birds may nest and rear their own chicks in aviary surroundings, but they usually prefer to parasitize firefinches. Like related birds, combassous are reasonably hardy once properly acclimatized, but it is usually best to bring them inside for the winter.

Family: PLOCEIDAE – Weavers and Sparrows
Confined to the Old World and closely related to the Viduinae, these birds
often build elaborate nests, some of which are woven in style.

Golden Song Sparrow
Passer luteus

● **Distribution:** Occurs over much
of northern Africa, from Nigeria east
to Sudan, Somalia, Ethiopia and
Arabia.
● **Size:** 12.5cm(5in).
● **Diet:** Foreign finch mix, with
greenfood and some livefood.
● **Sexing:** Cocks have bright
yellow plumage, whereas hens are
brownish overall.
● **Compatibility:** Agree well when
housed in groups.

In spite of their name, these birds
are not talented songsters; their
attraction lies in the sight of a
number of pairs housed together in
an aviary. Under these
circumstances they are more likely
to breed, since pairs show a greater

tendency to nest when kept in
groups. The beaks of cock birds
become noticeably darker at this
time. Although they will use a
nestbox, song sparrows are
generally keener to build their own
nests, lined with feathers, in a
suitable clump of gorse. Four
greenish white eggs form the usual
clutch, and these hatch after an
incubation period of 11 days.
Although livefood is not essential
for rearing purposes, offer it to the
birds if possible, along with
softfood and soaked seeds. The
chicks will fledge when only a
fortnight old; young birds resemble
hens until they moult out.

Below: **Golden Song Sparrow**
*The cock is yellow with chestnut
wings; the hen is brownish. Breed
these birds on a colony basis.*

Baya Weaver
Ploceus philippinus

- **Distribution:** From India across Southeast Asia.
- **Size:** 15cm(6in).
- **Diet:** Foreign finch mixture, with greenfood and some livefood.
- **Sexing:** Cock birds out of colour resemble hens, but lack yellow areas of plumage.
- **Compatibility:** Males may agree well when housed together, but can prove aggressive when paired.

In typical weaver fashion, these birds construct elaborate nesting chambers. Male birds start the building process, and hens add the finishing touches to a nest that, in the wild, may reach as much as 2.7m(9ft) in overall height! The birds enter the bulbous structure from beneath, via a long tubular tunnel, and lay between two and five eggs within. The incubation period lasts for a fortnight and at this stage the weavers avidly consume large quantities of livefood. Their chicks should leave the nest after a further two weeks.

Below: **Baya Weaver**
An Asiatic species that may attempt to build a very elaborate nesting site. Provide suitable material.

Red-billed Weaver
Quelea quelea

- **Distribution:** Occurs over most of Africa, south of the Sahara.
- **Size:** 12.5cm(5in).
- **Diet:** A mixture of the smaller cereal seeds, plus greenfood and livefood.
- **Sexing:** Cocks in colour have black, rather than brownish grey heads and a pinkish tinge to their plumage. Out of colour, males resemble hens, but often have darker markings.
- **Compatibility:** Do best when kept in groups.

The Red-billed Weaver is one of the commonest finches in Africa. Flocks of birds, sometimes numbering millions of individuals, are regarded as serious agricultural pests in many areas. Although these weavers are frequently available to the birdkeeper, breeding successes in aviary surroundings tend to be uncommon. This may well be because the birds need the stimulus of others of their own kind if they are to nest. Not surprisingly, therefore, they do best when housed as a group in a planted

Above: **Red-billed Weaver**
This species causes great damage in its native range, where huge flocks cause extensive damage to crops. Reasonably hardy.

Below: **Napoleon Weaver**
The cock bird's handsome yellow feathering is lost outside the breeding period. This species does not need colour feeding.

aviary. Nesting details are similar to those of the Baya Weaver. When breeding has occurred, the chicks have been reared with livefood.

In a few cases, the black coloration normally present on the face is replaced by reddish brown markings. Such birds are occasionally described as Russ's Weaver, although they are not officially accorded the status of a subspecies. The related Red-headed Quelea (*Quelea erythrops*) is sometimes available; it is more colourful than its Red-billed relative.

Napoleon Weaver
Euplectes afra

● **Distribution:** Occurs over most of Africa, south of the Sahara.
● **Size:** 12.5cm(5in).
● **Diet:** A mixture of the smaller cereal seeds, with greenfood and livefood.
● **Sexing:** Cocks in colour are recognizable by their yellow areas of plumage, whereas hens are predominantly brownish. Out of colour cocks resemble hens, but are less heavily marked, notably on the breast and flanks.
● **Compatibility:** Best kept in groups, or with birds of a similar or larger size.

In the wild, these weavers are said to favour a nesting site in a reed-bed, where they attach their nests to the rigid stems. The resulting structures are oval, with a side entrance located near the top of the nest. When breeding, the Napoleon Weaver may become territorial and the polygamous cock birds often prove aggressive towards other aviary occupants in defence of their nesting site. Provide a well-planted flight, with strands of bamboo for nesting purposes. The birds will need a supply of livefood, especially once their chicks have hatched. Up to four eggs form a typical clutch and the incubation and fledging periods both last about 14 days. The breeding habits of the Napoleon Weaver are similar to those of the Red Bishop.

105

Red Bishop
Euplectes orix

● **Distribution:** Ranges across northern Africa, from Senegal to Ethiopia and Tanzania, and south to Angola and South Africa.
● **Size:** 12.5cm(5in).
● **Diet:** A mixture of the smaller cereal seeds, plus greenfood and livefood.
● **Sexing:** Cocks in colour have characteristic orange markings. Out of colour, the plumage of both cock and hen is predominantly brown, although the cock may show a few black feathers.
● **Compatibility:** Keep a cock with several hens. Can be kept in an aviary with other weavers and birds of similar size.

Cocks of this species in nuptial plumage rank among the most colourful of the African finches. Colour feeding is recommended for the cock bird to maintain the depth of this reddish nuptial plumage. Various forms are recognized throughout their wide range.

They will nest successfully in aviary surroundings, especially when housed in a planted flight. Cocks are polygamous, so keep them with a small group of hens. Working with raffia, dried grasses and similar materials, the cock will construct a nesting chamber, thus attracting a hen to the site. As soon as she is settled, he repeats the process with another hen. Cocks, in fact, take no active part in the incubation phase or the rearing of chicks. A cock bird kept with just one hen may persecute the female during the breeding period, leading to losses of eggs or chicks. Remove young birds as soon as they are eating independently.

Below: **Red Bishop**
One of the most striking weavers in nuptial plumage. Eclipse plumage of both cock and hen is mainly brown.

White-winged Whydah
Euplectes albonatus

● **Distribution:** Eastern and southern parts of Africa, from the Sudan southwards.
● **Size:** Cocks in colour average 23cm(9in) in overall length, while hens measure 15cm(6in).
● **Diet:** A mixture of the smaller cereal seeds, plus greenfood and livefood.
● **Sexing:** Cocks in colour are more colourful than hens.
● **Compatibility:** Can be housed with other weavers and whydahs, but tend to do better when kept on their own.

The characteristic white areas of plumage on the wings, at the base of the primary feathers, give this species its common name. It is closely related to *E. macrocercus* the Yellow-shouldered Whydah.

Above: **White-winged Whydah**
One species that is not parasitic in its breeding habits. Provide livefood so that hens have a good chance of rearing their chicks.

Compared with the *Vidua* whydahs, White-winged Whydahs are not common avicultural subjects, and are potentially more aggressive as a group. For breeding purposes, therefore, house them on their own in a planted flight, with one cock to several hens.

Not all whydahs have parasitic breeding habits, as shown by this species. Its nesting habits are similar to those of the Napoleon Weaver and, if supplied with an adequate quantity of livefood, hens may successfully rear their own chicks. However, it is a good idea to remove the young whydahs as soon as you see that they are feeding independently.

Family: EMBERIZIDAE – Buntings and their allies
A relatively dull family in terms of coloration, although there are exceptions, certain members having very attractive markings. Again, the members of this family possess the typical short, compact beaks of seed-eating birds.

Black-crested Finch
Lophospingus pusillus

● **Distribution:** Bolivia, Paraguay and Argentina.
● **Size:** 12.5cm(5in).
● **Diet:** A canary seed mixture with added millet, as well as livefood and greenstuff.
● **Sexing:** Hens have grey rather than black crests and paler throats.
● **Compatibility:** May be aggressive, notably when breeding.

Although not commonly available, this species – sometimes described as the Pygmy Cardinal – settles well in aviary surroundings and pairs nest quite readily. The hen will often accept a canary nestpan, or even an open-fronted nestbox as a support for her rather flimsy attempts at nest-building. A typical clutch of two or three eggs should hatch within about 12 days, and livefood and softfood are vitally important for the successful rearing of the chicks. These fledge rapidly and normally leave the nest when barely two weeks old and before they are fully feathered. Because they leave the nest in a relatively immature state, the best chance of rearing chicks successfully is to house them in indoor flights. Out of doors, there is a greater risk that during periods of bad weather newly fledged birds will become saturated and fatally chilled. Once the chicks are eating independently, move them to separate quarters, as they may be persecuted by the cock, which is likely to be keen to breed again.

The Red-crested Finch (*Coryphospingus cucullatus*) is classified in another genus, but has similar requirements. It tends to spend much of its time close to the floor, especially when housed in a well-planted aviary.

Below: **Red-crested Finch**
An attractive species from South America. Unfortunately, it may not be widely available.

Red-crested Cardinal
Paroaria coronata

● **Distribution:** Southeastern Brazil, extending to Paraguay, Bolivia, Uruguay and northern Argentina.
● **Size:** 19cm(7.5in).
● **Diet:** A canary seed mixture, with softbill food and livefood, plus fruit and greenstuff.
● **Sexing:** No reliable visual distinctions possible, although hens are sometimes smaller.
● **Compatibility:** Pairs will prove aggressive when in breeding condition.

It is best to house these cardinals on their own in a well-planted aviary. They prefer to construct their nests without artificial supports, seeking out a suitable site in a shrub, often quite close to the ground. Using dried grass, moss and even small twigs, the hen builds the typical cup-shaped nest largely on her own. Here she will lay

Above: **Red-crested Cardinal**
Pairs will nest satisfactorily in a planted aviary, but they are likely to be aggressive towards other birds sharing their quarters.

three or four eggs, and incubate them alone for about a fortnight. Livefood is very important for the successful rearing of the chicks, which should fledge after a further two weeks. The hen may then lay again, while her mate takes over responsibility for the earlier chicks. They will be independent by the time they are a month old; ideally, remove them to separate accommodation at this stage.

Carefully acclimatize these cardinals before attempting to overwinter them in an outdoor aviary, and provide heat and light in their shelter in case the weather turns very severe. You should start colour feeding them before each moult, otherwise their fiery red head coloration may fade over the course of several years.

Rainbow Bunting
Passerina leclancheri

- **Distribution:** Mexico.
- **Size:** 12.5cm(5in).
- **Diet:** Canary seed mixture, with softbill food and livefood.
- **Sexing:** Hens are olive-green and lack the bright colours of cocks.
- **Compatibility:** Cocks tend to be aggressive, especially towards each other.

The *Passerina* buntings as a group are popular avicultural subjects, but have become much less common during recent years. The Rainbow Bunting is one of the most colourful species, but may prove difficult to establish, since it is more insectivorous in the wild than other species. Breeding attempts are further handicapped by the fact that hens are rarely available, since native trappers consider them less valuable than their colourful mates. Acclimatized, Rainbow Buntings will thrive in a planted aviary for the warmer part of the year, but may spend much of their time hidden in the vegetation. The hen builds a cup-shaped nest, and incubates her clutch of three or four eggs alone. These should hatch after a period of 12 days and, providing the chicks have had an adequate supply of livefood, they leave the nest after a similar interval.

Below: **Rainbow Bunting**
Cocks are especially colourful. Breeding buntings is difficult, since hens are rarely available.

Saffron Finch
Sicalis flaveola

- **Distribution:** Occurs over much of tropical South America, in lowland areas.
- **Size:** 15cm(6in).
- **Diet:** Canary seed mixture with added millets, plus livefood.
- **Sexing:** Hens are significantly duller than cocks.
- **Compatibility:** Can prove aggressive when breeding.

Eleven species of *Sicalis* finches are recognized by taxonomists; the Saffron Finch is probably the most widely kept in avicultural circles. Once they are established in their quarters, pairs will nest readily, choosing either a canary nestpan or an open-fronted nestbox for this purpose. The incubation and fledging periods both last about 14 days, and the young finches should be feeding themselves by the time they are a month old. At this stage you should transfer them to separate accommodation, since the adult birds will probably be nesting again. Soaked seed, invertebrates and seeding grasses are all valuable rearing foods; some pairs will even accept softbill food when they have chicks in the nest.

Collared Warbling Finch
Poospiza torquata

- **Distribution:** Bolivia and western Paraguay to northern and central parts of Argentina.
- **Size:** 12.5cm(5in).
- **Diet:** A foreign finch mixture, with softbill food, greenstuff and livefood.
- **Sexing:** Hens are usually paler in coloration than cocks.
- **Compatibility:** Tends to be aggressive, notably when breeding.

The warbling finches are not common avicultural subjects, and many of the 16 species are unknown in collections. They are not difficult birds to maintain, however, providing you can meet their specialist needs. In spite of

Above: **Saffron Finch**
*Pairs can be recognized quite easily
and will frequently attempt to nest
using a canary nestpan.*

their small size they are aggressive,
and cocks may even attack their
mates savagely. Keep them on their
own, therefore, in a planted aviary
and not as part of a mixed
collection. Furthermore, warbling
finches need to be kept warm
during the winter months, and
should be transferred to an indoor
flight over this period. Pairs will
often start nesting out of doors in
spring, building a cup-shaped nest
in a secluded area.

Three eggs form the typical
clutch, and these should hatch
within a fortnight. Provide plenty of
livefood to ensure that the chicks
are reared successfully. They may
leave the nest when only 12 days
old, and should be transferred to
separate quarters when feeding.

Left: **Collared Warbling Finch**
*These birds are not difficult to
maintain, but they need heated
indoor quarters over the winter.*

Cuban Finch
Tiaris canora

● **Distribution:** Cuba and the Isle of Pines (southwest of Cuba).
● **Size:** 10cm(4in).
● **Diet:** A foreign finch mixture, plus softbill food, greenstuff and livefood.
● **Sexing:** The yellow areas of plumage are much duller in hens.
● **Compatibility:** Keep individual pairs apart and house them separately from other species for greater breeding success.

Members of the genera *Volatinia* and *Tiaris* are sometimes described collectively as grassquits. This species has proved prolific in aviary surroundings, and is well established in aviculture. Cock birds tend to be aggressive towards each other, even when they are housed in adjoining flights, although two pairs have been housed together successfully in a well-planted aviary. Whereas the nest of the related Jacarini Finch *(Volatinia jacarina)* is cup-shaped the *Tiaris* grassquits build a domed nest in suitable vegetation within the aviary, using dried grasses. After laying her clutch of up to four eggs the hen sits alone, and the incubation period lasts for 12 days. Although these grassquits may take livefood when breeding, this does not appear to be essential for the successful rearing of chicks, especially if you provide other foods, such as soaked seed and greenfood. Chicks fledge at about two weeks old. After a further fortnight, when the young birds are feeding independently, remove them from their parents before they are persecuted by the cock.

Below: **Cuban Finch**
This grassquit builds a domed nest and may lay four eggs in a clutch. Livefood is not essential for the successful rearing of young.

Parrot-billed Seedeater

Sporophila peruviana

● **Distribution:** Arid coastal areas of Peru and Ecuador.
● **Size:** 10cm(4in).
● **Diet:** Foreign finch mixture with greenfood, such as seeding grasses and livefood.
● **Sexing:** Hens have a greyish rather than black area under the throat.
● **Compatibility:** Pairs are best kept on their own.

Although there are about 27 species of *Sporophila* seedeaters, they are not commonly seen in avicultural circles. Little has been recorded about many species, so there is plenty of scope for the birdkeeper who wants to pursue a specialized interest. Do not, however, confuse these finches with the African seed eaters, which belong to the genus *Serinus* and need similar care to that described for the singing finches (page 66).

As their common name suggests, these birds feed mainly on a diet of seeds, even when breeding. They are relatively

Above: **Parrot-billed Seedeater**
Named after the shape of the beak, Parrot-billed Seedeaters offer scope for breeders to specialize in a little-known group of birds.

undemanding in their feeding habits and do not require much livefood, although you should ensure that it is regularly available to them.

Seedeaters are not really suitable subjects for a mixed aviary containing waxbills, but you can house them alongside mannikins. However, under these conditions they are less likely to breed than if they are housed on their own. Unfortunately, hens are difficult to obtain, but an established pair of birds will usually attempt to breed in a planted flight.

The birds construct their nest low down in a suitable shrub, and the hen incubates the eggs on her own for about 12 days. The chicks leave the nest when they are a fortnight old and frequently conceal themselves for a few days on the floor of the aviary. At this stage you must ensure that the youngsters do not become soaked or chilled in a shower of rain.

Index to species

Page numbers in **bold** indicate major references, including accompanying photographs. Page numbers in *italics* indicate captions to other illustrations. Less important text entries are shown in normal type.

A

African Silverbill **94**
Alario finches 51
Amadina erythrocephala 99
   A. fasciata **99**
Amandava amandava 82
   A. formosa **82–3**
   A. subflava **83**
Amblyospiza albifrons 50
Aurora Finch **72**, 73
Australian finches 42, *49*, 50, 52, 53, 54, 56

B

Baya Weaver, **104**, 105
Bengalese Finch 26, 52, *53*, 53, *54*, 54, 56, 62, **96–7**
   Albino 96
   Fawn and White *97*
   Pied 96, *97*
   Self Chestnut 96
   Self Chocolate 96, *97*
   Self Fawn *96*, 96
Bicheno Finch *53*, **88**
Black-bellied Seedcracker **74**
Black-cheeked Waxbill 80
Black-crested Finch **108**
Black-headed Nun 92
Bluebills 73
Blue-breasted Cordon Bleu **77**, 77
Blue-capped Cordon Bleu 77
Blue-faced Parrot-finch **91**
Bronze-winged Mannikin **94–5**
Bullfinches 37, 69
Buntings 10, 64, **108–113**

C

Cardinals 41
Carduelis carduelis **68**
   C. carduelis caniceps 69
   C. chloris **67**
Chestnut-breasted Mannikin *14*
Chestnut Munia 92
Chestnut Nun 92
Chinese Hawfinch 70
Chinese Painted Quail 84
Chloebia gouldiae **89**
Coccothraustes coccothraustes **70**
   C. migratoria 70
   C. personatus 70
Collared Warbling Finch **110–111**
Common Bullfinch **69**
Common Hawfinch **70**
Common Waxbill 81
Cordon Bleu Waxbill 50
Coryphospingus cucullatus **108**, 108
Crimson-rumped Waxbill *36*
Cuban Finch **112**
Cut-throat 52, **99**

D

Diamond Firetail 50, **84–5**
Diamond Sparrow 84
Dybowski's Twin-spot 75

E

Emberizidae 64, **108–113**
Emblema guttata 84
Erythrura prasina **90**
   E. trichroa **91**
Estrilda astrild 81
   E. caerulescens **79**
   E. charmosyna 80
   E. erythronotos 80
   E. melpoda **80–1**
   E. rhodopyga *36*
   E. troglodytes **82**
Estrildidae 64, **71–99**
Euplectes afra **105**
   E. albonatus **107**
   E. macrocercus 107
   E. orix **106**
European Goldfinch **68–9**
Euschistospiza dybowskii 75
Excalfactoria chinensis 84

F

Firefinch 102
Fringillidae 10, 37, 64, **66–70**

G

Giant Green Singing Finch 67
Gold-breasted Waxbill *47*, **83**
Golden Song Sparrow **103**
Gouldian Finch 13, 50, 52, *53*, 55,
   Black-headed *13*, 89
   Immature *13*
   Lutino 56
   Red-headed *15*, 89
   Yellow-headed *89*, 89
Green Avadavat **82–3**
Greenfinch 13, **67**
   Lutino *Endpapers*, 67
Green-backed Twin-spot 75
Green Munia 82
Green Singing Finch *45*, **66**
Green-winged Pytilia **72–3**
Grey-headed Olive-back **71**
Grey-headed Silverbill 95
Grey Singing Finch **66–7**

H

Hawfinches 14
Himalayan Goldfinch 69
Hypargos niveiguttatus **75**

I

Indian Silverbill 94
Indigo bird 102

J

Jacarini Finch 112
Jameson's Firefinch *Title page*
Japanese Hawfinch 70
Java Sparrow 46, **98**

L

Lagonosticta senegala 76
Lavender Finch 79
Lonchura atricapilla 92
　L. caniceps 95
　L. castaneothorax 14
　L. cucullata 94–5
　L. domestica 96
　L. fringilloides 95
　L. maja 92
　L. malabarica cantans 94
　L.m. malabarica 94
　L. malacca 92
　L. oryzivora 98
　L. punctulata 93
　L. striata 96
Long-tailed Grassfinch 88–9
　Heck's Contents page, 88, 89
　Yellow-billed 88
Lophospingus pusillus 108

M

Magpie Mannikin 95
Mandingoa nitidula 75
　M.n. schlegeli 75
Mannikins 46, 63, 64, 71, 113
Masked Grassfinch 89
Melba Finch 72–3
Munias 46, 63, 64, 71, 99

N

Napoleon Weaver 105, 107
Negro Finches 71
Nesocharis capistrata 71
Nigrita sp. 71
Nutmeg Finch 93

O

Orange-cheeked Waxbill 64–5, 80–1
Ortygosiza atricollis 84
Owl Finch 88

P

Pale-headed Munia 92
Paroaria coronata 109
Parrot-billed Seedeater 113
Parson's Finch 88
Passer luteus 103
Passerina leclancheri 110
Pearl-headed Silverbill 95
Peter's Twin-spot 75
Pink-bellied Waxbill 80
Pin-tailed Nonpareil 90
Pin-tailed Whydah 101
Ploceidae 64, 103–107
Ploceus philippinus 104
Poephila acuticauda 88–9
　P.a. hecki 88
　P. bichenovii 88
　P. cincta 88, 89
　P. guttata 86–7
　P. personata 89
　P. ruficauda 85
Poospiza torquata 110–111
Purple Grenadier Waxbill 78
Pygmy Cardinal 108

Pyrenestes ostrinus 74
Pyrrhula pyrrhula 69
　P.p. cineracea 69
　P.p. pyrrhula 69
Pytilia melba 72–3
　P. phoenicoptera 72

Q

Quail Finch 48, 84
Queen Whydah 100
Quelea erythrops 105
　Q. quelea 104–5

R

Rainbow Bunting 110
Red Avadavat 60, 61, 82–3, 83
Red-billed Weaver 104–5
Red Bishop 50, 105, 106
Red-cheeked Cordon Bleu 76–7
Red-crested Cardinal 109
Red-crested Finch 10–11, 108, 108
Red-eared Cordon Bleu 82
Red-eared Waxbill 82
Red-headed Finch 99
Red-headed Quelea 105
Red-winged Pytilia 72
Rice Bird 98
Russ's Weaver 105

S

Saffron Finch 110
St. Helena Seedeater 67
St. Helena Waxbill Half-title page, 81
Schlegel's Twin-spot 75
Senegal Combassou 47, 102
Senegal Firefinch 76
Serinus alario 51
　S. atrogularis 67
　S. canarius 66
S. flaviventris 67
　S. leucopygius 66–7
　S. mozambicus 66
Siberian Bullfinch 69
Sicalis flaveola 110
Society Finch 54, 96
Sparrows 64, 103–107
Spermophaga haematina 73
Spice Finch 93
Sporophila peruviana 113
Star Finch 85
　Albino 85
　Yellow-headed 85
Sundevall's Waxbill 36

T

Thick-billed Weaver 50
Tiaris canora 112
Tiger Finch 82
Tri-coloured Nun 92

U

Uraeginthus angolensis 77
　U. bengalus 76–7
　U. cyanocephalus 77
　U. granatina 78
　U. ianthinogaster 78

V

Vidua chalybeata **102**
  V. macroura **101**
  V. regia **100**
Vidua sp. 101, 102, 107
Viduinae 64, **100–102**, 103
Violet-eared Waxbill 51, **78**, 100
Virginian Cardinal *41*
Volatinia jacarina 112

W

Waxbills 32, 46, 64, 71, 99, 100, 101,
  102
Weavers 13, 41, 46, 49, 50, 63, 64
  Parasitic **100–102**
  Non-parasitic **103–107**
Western Bluebill **73**
White-backed Munia 96
White-headed Mannikin 92
White-headed Nun *63*, **92**, 93, 95

White-winged Whydah **107**
Whydahs 46, 64, **100–102**

Y

Yellow-rumped Serin 67
Yellow-shouldered Whydah 107

Z

Zebra Finch 30, 39, *46*, 46, 56, 86–7
  Albino 86
  Black-breasted *57*
  Chestnut-flanked White (CFW) 86, *87*
  Cream 87
  Crested *87*, 87
  Fawn 87
  Fawn Pied 87
  Orange-breasted *57*
  Phaeo *57*
  Pied 87
  Silver 87
  White *86*

Further reading

Alderton, D. *Looking after Cage birds* Ward Lock, 1982, 1987
Alderton, D. *Beginner's Guide to Zebra Finches* Paradise Press, 1984
Alderton, D. *The Complete Cage and Aviary Bird Handbook* Pelham
  Books, 1986
Arnall, L & Keymer, I.F. *Bird Diseases* Baillere Tindall, 1975
Goodwin, D. *Estrildid Finches of the World* British Museum (Natural
  History), 1983
Harper, D. *Pet Birds for Home and Garden* Salamander Books, 1986
Immelmann, K. *Australian Finches* Angus and Robertson, 1982
Martin, R.M. *Cage and Aviary Birds* Collins, 1980
Mobbs, A. *Gouldian Finches* Nimrod, 1985
Restall, R.L. *Finches and other Seed-eating Birds* Faber and Faber, 1975
Rutgers, A. & Norris, K.A. (editors) *Encyclopedia of Aviculture* (Volume III)
  Blandford Press, 1977
Trollope, J. *The Care and Breeding of Seed-eating Birds* Blandford Press,
  1983

Picture credits

Artists
Copyright of the artwork illustrations on the pages following the artists'
names is the property of Salamander Books Ltd.

John Francis: 20–21, 23, 25, 28–29, 58

Alan Harris: 46

Seb Quigley: 31

Photographs
Unless otherwise stated, all the photographs have been taken by and are
the copyright of Cyril Laubscher. The publishers wish to thank the following
photographers who have supplied other photographs for this book. The
photographs have been credited by page number and position on the page:
(B)Bottom, (T)Top, (C)Centre, (BL)Bottom left etc.

B.H. Coles: 59

Acknowledgements
The publishers wish to thank the following for their help in preparing this
book: Viv Anderson; Paul and June Bailey; Eric Barlow; Fred Barnicoat; Neil
Bloxham; Sharon Burrell; George Coe; Andrew Cripps; Mick and Marion
Cripps; Alan Donnelly; Ray Fisk; Jeff Foreman; Brian Gibbs; Dave and Sue
Gillam; Rodney and Joan Hamilton; George Lewsey; Gordon Little; Stanley
Maughan; Doug Neill; Phyllis Nicholas; Ron Oxley; Mike and Jane
Pickering; Mick and Beryl Plose; Porter's Cage Bird Appliances; Janet and
Alan Ralph; Judy Raven; Ron Rayner; Val Read; Ronpet Pet Shop; Dave
Russell; Keith Ruth; Raymond Sawyer; Stuart Shillinglaw; Tony Smith;
Josef Somers; Terry Stevenson; Peter Thumbwood; Graham Tulk; Joyce
Venner; Cliff Wright; Tony and Jean Youe. Rita Hemsley (for typing the
author's manuscript).

Lutino Greenfinch